The Universal Language of Nature

The Universal Language of Nature

*A New Way of Conflict Resolution
and Authentic Leadership*

Alexandra Sitch

HybridGlobal
PUBLISHING

Published by
Hybrid Global Publishing
301 E. 57th Street, 4th floor
New York, NY 10022

Manufactured in the United States of America,
or in the United Kingdom when distributed elsewhere.

Sitch, Alexandra
The Universal Language of Nature:
A New Way of Conflict Resolution and Authentic Leadership
ISBN: 978-1-951943-08-0
eBook: 978-1-951943-09-7
LCCN: 2020905411

Cover design by: Jonathan Pleska
Copyediting by: Lara Kennedy
Interior design: Medlar Publishing Solutions Pvt Ltd., India
Author photo by: Galina Ivanova Photography (@fotoformemories)

www.sitchmediation.com

I am a citizen, not of Athens or Greece, but of the world.
Socrates

Which universal aspects connect different
peoples and cultures?

Every new solution to a problem goes through
three phases in society: you laugh at it, you fight it,
and then it's taken for granted.
Nicholas Klein

Table of Contents

Prologue 1

From a macro world to a micro world 7

Maybe a new software: "Solomon's Ring 2.0" to be
    in tune with nature 13

In nature 17

A new universal element is added to my professional life 21

A turbulent way to myself, or a traumatic love 27

The methodology 31

The masks for survival 33

Schizoid mask: "The airballoon into the clouds" 35

Oral mask: The human who never has enough 37

Symbiotic mask 39

Rigid mask 41

Psychopathic mask 43

Masochistic mask 45

The paths to harmony 49

Germany 55

Not everything is as it seems 61

A team: Process tweaking or human potential? 67

France 71

Success in professional life: The question behind the question 77

"First love" in a session with a French couple 83

Italy 85

The bully in a love relationship 87

Controlled first love. 89

Israel 91

A world between words. 95

The absent father 97

How connected are we?. 101

What exactly is the feeling of "inner wisdom"? 105

A fragmented world in search of "complement". 109

Are not these all very current sayings in this day and age?. 115

Mediation: Solve conflicts with empathy and logic 117

Mediation or public diplomacy in society and politics 121

Lack of empathy development in education:
      "An avalanche is approaching us" 129

How horses react to self-love 133

A little exercise for you, this time without horses 135

The big field: Horses show us tendencies and energy
      in today's society. 137

Tranquility 143

Dark and light 145

Bibliography. 149

Prologue

"I DO NOT FEEL valued in my office, and decisions are quite often made behind my back," the manager said.

He stood in the middle of the herd of horses, which stood clearly far away from each other, without any visible contact, representing his colleagues and the atmosphere on his team. One horse stood next to him, petrified and seemingly "logged out," representing himself.

He recognized his boss, the general director, in another horse who was walking away, disconnected from his team and focusing on his life outside the team.

Throughout the conversation with this client, it became clear that the business culture in his company was not a very constructive one. Colleagues were often bullied, the communication within the team was not clear, and the general director seemed to avoid going into the issues this manager brought up during meetings.

The outcome of the exercise was clear; the best way to resolve his concerns was getting into contact with his boss and bringing across his point of view on current matters. It required more of his self-confidence and crystal-clear communication.

I asked him to walk toward his boss, represented by the horse, and tell him what bothered him the most. He took a step toward his boss, the distracted horse, and expressed his concern.

The horse still seemed to be uninterested and turned away his head. I asked the manager if he felt confident enough in expressing his feelings. He reacted surprised; never in his life had he wondered about his way of communicating. Probably he was not really focused enough on what he wanted to say. He admitted that he still doubted himself

Once he had filled himself with confidence, after a small breathing exercise and with authenticity, he opened his mouth and expressed his desire for communication to be clear between the two of them.

The horse took a step toward him, and the rest of the herd came closer as well.

Synergy on a team and authentic leadership are first of all dependent on human factors. If people have not found their place in the company and the level of clear empathic communication is minimal, a company can never show good results in the long run.

In business, the goal has so far been clearly defined: it is mostly about generating profits, with many businesses unfortunately forgetting the important influence of private life on working life. As in the case described, a company suffers when there is lack of engagement or absenteeism.

And the ever-increasing digitalization of society will also have consequences: are human values and sustainability sufficiently applied? Should important human skills be considered in the process? Or are people divided according to dualistic criteria that categorize a person as either bad or good?

What people want more and more in their life is freedom, the freedom to be oneself in order to develop one's own abilities. Is not this the need of most people, to have the freedom to develop authentically, with empathy for themselves and for others, without judgment or conditioning in all areas of life? In what ways can we be helped?

The biggest trauma of humanity is probably the giving up of intuition, the critical mind. I am sure that many of this generation recognize themselves here. Many have grown up with a kind of conditioning that has been shaped by world wars, the processing of traumas, victim and attacker complexes, social conventions, and general societal expectations; for example, the idea that one "advances" and climbs the social ladder. One gains capital to be considered by the outside world as "correct," often detached from personal authenticity and universal ethics.

Sue was a dynamic marketing manager and worked with several colleagues in a team. When she contacted me she mentioned her burnout problems and told me that she had had to remain at home for several weeks up until now because of this. She was wondering what to do and whether it was a good idea to return to her rather stressful work in the same company.

Almost total silence had fallen around the stables when Sue chose her place in the middle of the ring. She stood there silently and a 'heavy' atmosphere was evident. The horses had walked away from her and now stood close to the walls on the periphery and appeared blocked in their demeanor. They seemed even petrified, as though they would fall to the ground at any moment.

I asked Sue what she saw and what she was experiencing. She mentioned the stress and the burden, and noticed that this was clearly reflected both in the behavior of the horses, and in the demanding atmosphere encountered in her company. 'Our business culture is tough and competitive' she stated. All the while she looked very sad.

I asked her with which horse she was able to identify the most.

'The one there in the back looking outside the ring as if he wants to escape and nearly collapsing on the floor. It is exactly how I feel nowadays!'

'Do you believe a desire to 'escape' is behind the reason for your burnout?' I asked her. She did not answer immediately.

There was no sound when suddenly my dog, which had been sitting quietly outside the ring, started barking and ran towards her in a lively, playful manner. The dog sat down next to her, but did not stop barking. Animals always interact with other animals and respond to the energy of the so-called 'knowing field'.

I asked her what this dog reminded her of. She started to sob. 'My own dog died a few months ago, and at about the same time I heard from the hospital that I had breast cancer'.

Once Sue had acknowledged her inner feelings, the dog ceased its restless behavior and sat down next to her; the particular horse Sue had been most able to identify with walked over to her and put its nose against her belly, constituting a representation of people's intuition and emotions.

It is common but not widely known that animals are able to sense the presence of a question behind a question. 'Should I go back to the same competitive company?' was in fact replaced by a more fundamental question, namely 'Have I taken sufficient care of myself, my grief, my health, and of what I really want in life?'.

At this point I suggested to Sue to properly make contact with her horse. In doing so, she effectively brought herself back into contact with herself, and this reminded her of the necessity to grief about the loss of her dog and to come to terms with her disease. She buried her face in the warm coat of the horse.

At this point I suggested to Sue to properly make contact with her horse. In doing so, Sue effectively brought herself back into contact with herself, and this reminded her of the necessity to grief about the loss of her dog and to come to terms with her disease. She buried her face in the warm coat of the horse.

The horse put Sue in a foal position, hiding her from sight so she could have this vulnerable private moment to herself, and she let her tears run freely.

After a while, the horse made a step sideways to let Sue speak with us again, as if it was able to feel when the timing was right. She looked at me and spoke spontaneously.

'That did me the power of good. Whilst yet to decide, I feel I should not go back to the same company since I need space for myself; I have felt terribly lonely until this point'.

The other horses walked towards her, as if they then noticed that they could see her as she really was and respected her place in life. The dog stayed quietly on the floor by her side, as if representing her own deceased companion.

A few months later she told me that she then felt much better, having left her old company with its toxic environment, and physically and emotionally had found a better balance, and recently started her own company giving her greater overall satisfaction.

From a macro world
to a micro world

ON SUNDAY EVENING, STEPHEN is sitting in his villa. He's just back from a luxury vacation in Madagascar. There he spent a week with his wife amid a fabulous vista of nature by the pool. Unfortunately, his wife did not talk to him much, which did not really bother him as long as he could work in peace, with his iPad there for him to answer his emails, and think about his new Bayliner. For calls, he had switched his phone on forwarding to his office. Nevertheless, he had the feeling that he still had to work on some projects, even on vacation, especially because his team members seemed overstrained or not motivated. One of his staff had been ill for some time. Stephen quickly sent him a message over WhatsApp: "Get well soon, Brad!"

He was already lucky with the rest of the gifted staff, who could cover his work.

Despite his professional success, his wealth, a wonderful family—his sons had just received their academic grades—and a promising future, Stephen felt exhausted after this holiday. He sensed that he was less fortunate in the private sphere and that his wife had become a stranger to him. He did not know himself anymore.

How many people can recognize themselves in Stephen? Life is so fast and full of routine. It's like living in a matrix, where one's place is determined by the system's rules and expectations, protocols, pressures, and deadlines.

Yes, we live in a world of confusion, due to globalization and digital development. We all have access to sophisticated technology. This brings us many advantages but unfortunately also increasingly creates a very fragmented world. If we need assistance from a help desk, we get an options menu with A, B, or C; however, if no adequate option is available, there is often no way to talk to someone. There are rules and laws for every system we work with. But are the true "laws of life" being considered at all?

We are all used to communicating on multiple social platforms, such as Facebook, LinkedIn, Instagram, and the like, keeping in touch with our social environment—with friends and family or colleagues. We write comments on posts and distribute many "likes." Somehow this has become the norm, just to establish a pseudo-esteem for someone. At the same time, we like to post pictures to show the world how successful, interesting, and appreciated we are, at least how we would like to see ourselves, without getting involved in a deeper conversation and listening to the other actively and with interest. But perhaps you would like to express your own feelings more honestly and authentically.

Most companies work with advanced management solutions. These are often processes that focus on optimizing communication by "forcing" people into a matrix full of logarithms to increase efficiency, without paying attention to individual needs. Instead of pursuing recognition and appreciation and companies which focus on financial resources, personal development with individual goals and ambitions could have a motivating effect. As such, we are thus hindered by unconscious emotional blockages. These are emotional scars and beliefs that come from childhood and the family system and have shaped our experiences. These unconscious beliefs and patterns are unfortunately often negatively affected and as self-fulfilling prophecies are then affecting several areas of life. They express themselves through interference in communication in our relationships and thus have a negative impact on the team's synergy, on the optimal functioning of a company, and even on society.

In a study by Dr. Travis Bradberry, as far as emotional intelligence and empathy for employees is concerned, researchers found that managers from middle management still perform well enough in terms of emotional intelligence and empathy for the employee—and of course for him- or herself. But in top management, the results of emotional intelligence tests are alarmingly poor.

Of all the people followed at work, it was found that 90% of top performers are also high in emotional intelligence. On the flip side, just 20% of bottom performers are high in emotional intelligence. This would mean you can be a top performer without emotional intelligence, but the chances are slim.

The assumption here is that the manager with a high EQ (also called Emotional Intelligence—EI) is the one that employees like to work with. But, as stated, the situation changes drastically if we compare the situation in middle management with that in higher management.

For directors and other senior executives, the results of the EQ test are drastically decreasing; CEOs generally have the lowest EQ results in the field. But it is a fact that the CEOs with the best performance in business are the ones with the highest EQ. You may be able to earn a PhD with a low EQ, but you will do less well in performing your management tasks!

In business, the lack of connection between people and within teams, and the lack of appreciation and emotional intelligence among managers, results in unpleasant consequences.

An unmotivated team achieves fewer positive results. Employees often feel left alone, and bullying—as experienced already in school—is unfortunately no exception. Those who experienced it at school take the experience and behavior resulting from that into their professional life. That is why an empathic manager and systemic coaching for teams are imperative to analyze and optimize the dynamics for sustainable business success.

A study-essay by Tiffany Jones says the following about this:

Many managers engage in destructive behavior. Destructive behavior and the toxicity to others can do harm not only to other employees and the organization, but also to themselves. Managers who are narcissistic, unethical, rigid or aggressive, make working with them extremely difficult for others. Managers can ultimately cause serious damage to their organizations because they divert the good performance of others to decreased cooperation, a weakened morale and hurting other's performance, which all lead to poor business decisions as a manager (Lubit, 2004). Managers with low EI do not have the ability themselves to promote a healthy EI within the workplace, which leads to minimal existence of EI presented by employees as well. (from *The Lack of Emotional Intelligence in the Workplace Business Essay*)

Modern man has somehow lost track of the big picture, of his sense of context and relationships, and under these circumstances, he continues to carry his frustrations through life. He adapts to a kind of fast-food culture and ignores the essentials of life. After just two years of senior specialist experience, we are considered experts in one area but are only focused on fragments. This is the case in private life as well. Depression and burnout, as well as physical problems or illnesses, are possible consequences and not infrequently a sign that the personality and/or feelings in the person's life have not received the necessary attention.

Maybe a new software: "Solomon's Ring 2.0" to be in tune with nature

MANY MANAGERS DO NOT feel well at all within their work and are full of stress; somehow, they can no longer cope with their colleagues, their deadlines, and the time pressure and thus have no private life, much less a happy one. Meanwhile, they must forcefully present themselves as a kind of rendition of Steve Jobs or at least want that role—even though deep down, they consider it a farce. Is it just a lack of competence? Are they with the wrong company after all? Or are there too many bottlenecks in the team?

Let's look at the scene with Stephen:

His footsteps made a soft springing sound on the earthy ground of the forest, the scattered sunlight shining through the yellowish foliage of the trees. Only some twittering of birds and the hum of a distant car could be heard. Stephen had left his office after the meeting with the team; the main topic was, again, the agile management system. He was most worried about the frictions in the sales team and the arguments about the best method. One of his employees, out of anger, said nothing during the whole session and just stared in front of him. These unpleasant conflicts had already had consequences for some customers; moreover, a big mistake in processing had caused customer loss due to change of producer.

During the meeting, Stephen had received several messages from his wife asking for her to get a prescription from the doctor. She had suffered from anxiety attacks for some time and hoped for some improvement due to new medication.

When Stephen arrived home, his wife was in tears and angry at his unassuming attitude. She complained, "You treat me like one of your employees. You're not talking to me at all! What do you expect from life? I only have contact with you via cell phone or iPad, and you do not even notice me! I could as well have gone on vacation alone!" She slammed the front door behind her and disappeared around the corner in her Porsche.

There was a feeling of anger in Stephen. He had always been generous with her, always buying her the most beautiful and elegant things. How dare she talk to him like that!

They had met each other a long time ago at the tennis club. At that time, they shared many hobbies and made plans together. All this had faded, unnoticed and pushed into the background; over time, their joint activities became less and less. Stephen had bought this company, worked hard, and had a lot of success with his good team and in the booming market. But these were not good times for both of them.

Stephen looked through the trees and saw some happy-to-play starlings flying through the branches, while a magpie nearby made a cackling noise. All these birds seemed to have found their place in life and did not wonder if they were doing it right; they were just there and took part in life. Stephen felt that he could relax a bit at the sight and distance himself from the day's conflicts. Didn't a good friend say to him: "In nature you have the best connection"?

Of course, sales should be realized and business data should be controlled, but how can one feel optimal in spite of daily burdens and get the right balance to master everything? Despite the prevalence of management courses, or new control gadgets that make it all a lot easier, it's hard to find values like empathy; appreciation and dialogues, such as using nurture words as an expression of the appreciation of a colleague; and freedom and leisure time in order to simply be human. Maintaining a healthy world of feelings, a secure balance of one's inner self, makes people more motivated, inspired, and creative in finding solutions, and they deliver higher performance. Many studies clearly show that reducing working hours makes employees much more motivated, engaged, and efficient. Achievements are thus realized faster, and goals are still met.

To establish this balance, we need the connection with ourselves. And where do we find this best? ...

In nature

THERE, WHERE WE FEEL free, uncomplicated, and accepted, one immediately notices that it makes a difference—especially in whether a conversation is conducted in the office or outside. Why are many team-building sessions being organized outdoors, in nature? Why are more and more companies wanting to be associated with nature and increasingly with sustainability?

Sustainability is not only respect for nature and the environment but also respect for people and their human, ethical values. It seems that somehow we feel that we need more "soft" tools in business and in society, not only because the law requires it or because it is trendy, but because we feel and sense more and more that a purely profit-oriented society, in which only performance and money count, is not fulfilling enough to us.

Every human, every creature, seeks balance and harmony

We can learn a lot from nature: everything is part of a larger whole and has a function and a place in life. Animals act according to their instincts and their senses in an interconnected way. This is a natural system in which man also participates and with which he is associated, only he has long since forgotten this and thus his own place in life. Animals know their place; they ask no questions and live their lives, instinctively aware of their function. Scientific studies show that they have sensitivity; they know, feel, and hear much more than today's human beings. This makes them part of a larger reality.

Horses, for example, have always lived in herds and never lost that group feeling, even in their stables. The herd always stood for safety and survival. This given can be used in coaching—especially for management-related topics. Every single horse, with its individual qualities, is of importance to the whole group; with its function, it occupies an important place in the hierarchy. If a horse is weakened, according to several studies, the other horses will compensate and support this weaker link in the herd. It is therefore also in the interest of the whole group that every horse uses its full potential. Interestingly, the other horses help the weaker one through a mix of body language and vibration to accomplish this goal.

On top of that, humans still have their brains. Obviously, our dynamic society, supported by well-thought-out systems that usually allow, predominantly, only one-sided gains, has taken over and/or neglected or pushed into the background the feeling of emotional intelligence that goes beyond verbal exchanges. Thus, in our modern society, unfortunately, man has somehow lost the possibility of coming into contact with his intuition, his gut feeling, and applying it positively.

This makes it harder to develop and use our authentic potential to get in better touch with ourselves and others and thus respond more adequately to situations and clearly feel how strongly we all depend on one another. The loss or failure of a group or partnership automatically has consequences to ourselves. The ideal condition for changing would be to rejoin the intuition, bringing emotional intelligence back to the mind.

Every culture has its own stage

For many years, I worked at companies within the field of intercultural communication in Europe and Asia. It was exciting to feel and participate in this diversity. Thanks to my multicultural background, I understood the different social norms of behavior and languages and could feel at home in several cultures. While working in France, I felt that I was part of French culture, where I often talked about vision and negotiated the process of development. In Germany, on the other hand, I had to adapt to the more formal system of manners, in which one endeavors to reach the goal within a short time.

At the same time, however, I wanted to nurture my humanistic thoughts and increasingly seek communication in terms of universal values—such as respect and equal rights—in order to achieve a kind of unity in diversity. I noticed that a bird's-eye view gave me the opportunity to relativize annoying situations with people because of rigid national attitudes or systemic social codes.

Another feeling became more and more prominent with me: words in a conversation are only part of the communication, or "communicating energy," between people. The nonverbal message, the tone, the underlying beliefs, and the intentions are not necessarily worded but nevertheless also play an extremely important role. Didn't you sometimes have the feeling that all factually important things were said in a dialogue, but somehow you did not get to the core and left with a slight feeling of dissatisfaction?

Gradually, I became more involved in the realm of mediation, resolving conflict situations, and preventive coaching to avoid conflicts between parties and teams. Instead of spending money on expensive legal procedures, which often only lead to frustration and a poorer relationship with the other party, a communication process is initiated in which one engages and listens to the other's motives.

The fact that both sides are heard and understood enables the development of a solution. Often, however, the same conflicts arise again; then the cause is much deeper. Some conflicts come from education, from the system in which one grew up; this happens unconsciously but later has a great impact on one's ability to resolve a conflict. The projecting of fear, anger, and guilt and consequent conflicts within oneself must be solved first.

Mediation techniques and coaching methods are mainly based on solution possibilities by means of the mind. These are well-thought-out theories and strategies, but the unconscious, the emotional world, is largely ignored. This happens especially in the areas where misinterpretations and unconscious feelings are stored as a result of a family "system." But these feelings are the real obstacles in conflict resolution.

I myself was the product of education, where intellectual development and academic degrees were important and the intuitive was secondary. But some events in my private life changed my view of the world and at the same time gave me new possibilities.

A new universal element is added to my professional life

⁓

IN DEMANDING WORK, YOU need healthy boundaries to keep your balance and enough time to spend on activities and people you like. Since my childhood, I had a great love for horses, and I started horse-riding lessons early. I felt respect, sometimes even awe, for these animals, but they gave me a sense of freedom and gave me very positive energy, even when I was not in a good mood.

On my fortieth birthday, I finally managed to afford a horse: Quieto, a horse that gave me the impression of being a philosopher, without stress, with gentle eyes. With the speed of a sports car, he galloped happily along the seashore with me.

After some time, I adopted an Andalusian named Juan, who was like a brother to Quieto, and the two became inseparable over time and stood together peacefully in their pen. Whenever I had time, I put them both out on the lawn of the ranch, an open area that went into the wild garigue landscape where the ranch owner's horses grazed.

One day when they stood with the others in the middle of the green meadow, another horse owner came to me. She was a little confused and told me that she wanted to put her horse here, too, but was afraid to let it in with the others. I told her that they understood each other very well and that I stayed there to keep an eye on the situation. She got even more agitated and started attacking me. At that moment, Quieto ran to us and stood between the young woman and me. I was with him in the foal position, which serves to protect from other horses in nature. He seemed to sense that I was in a vulnerable position at the time and wanted to create a balance by interposing. It was only after I relaxed again that I said to her, over Quieto's back, "I'm sorry, but we can discuss everything later." After that, Quieto moved and stood behind us; he bowed his head and gently touched her and my hand as if to bring them together. It gave the situation something surreal, and the tension gradually subsided.

Sometime after this event, I understood more and more that horses immediately feel our energy and relationships and want to reestablish a balance with gestures so that each of us will become aware of their authentic power.

An organized fair I attended that focused on equine-assisted life and management coaching confirmed my idea, and I was convinced that this could be the missing element in mediation and coaching practice, which I recognized from my mediation and conflict activities. During many sessions, I learned about the limits of the mind and began to read more and more about psychology and the positive influence of nature. How could one stimulate emotional intelligence, make more use of the senses, and give universal value to sessions within different cultural contexts? This was obviously possible for people with a variety of topics and systemic backgrounds.

It felt like all the puzzle pieces finally fit together; my intercultural interest related to interpersonal psychology, the intellect with intuition, the emotional world and empathy, nature and horses with humanity.

In fact, I did some specialized literature-research about animal behavioral science shortly thereafter. Norbert Sachser, a leading animal behavioral scientist, in his book *Der Mensch im Tier* (The Human Animal), mentions that mammals learn and communicate at a high level, that animals have a personality, and that a revolution in how we view animals is in full swing.

But he also mentions that as far as the scientific study of emotions is concerned, behavioral biology is just beginning, whereas models make predictions that can only be subsequently verified in empirical studies and further explored.

Within two years, I learned to understand the language of horses through very different situations between horses and humans and to interpret them for the benefit of humans, as well as the rest of nature, which interacts at the same time. This is an exceptional help in coaching people. A horse can only respond in a systemic way. It reveals the whole picture and the systemic background of a person you work with. It deals directly with the essence and the "life theme" of the human being, always in the present and without judgment.

In a herd of horses, where every horse has a place, it is most important that every horse takes its place. All will ensure that they use their full potential, otherwise one's weakness must and therefore will be compensated for. The same applies to humans; as soon as a person places himself within a group of horses, the horses will regard him or her as part of the group and immediately sense the personality, the communicative energy, and the relationships of that person, representing his or her family or professional system in a kind of *tableau vivant*, or role-play, in order for that person to become self-reliant to free him- or herself from the family system and from other mental obstructions.

Any inner mental or straight emotional movement of the human being will change the reactions of the horse, and it will then lead the person to the next step of his or her development. Thus, we have the opportunity to treat varying questions and life issues during a systemic therapy or coaching session with horses: since the horses live only in the present, in the now, they always show us what is most important at a particular moment. Moreover, another horse, participant, or symbolic anchor can represent certain persons or themes in a person's life story. Interestingly enough, as a representative, even another human being can sense the energy of the person or element represented and as such provide additional information. A fascinating world opens up in which every human immediately recognizes and feels his or her system and background.

In this process, we also work with the language and the signals of the horses, a language with movements and actions that, according to nature, have their own meaning and contain many nuances, depending on the context or personal gut feeling of the person. I would like to briefly describe a few examples in which *reflective* horse coaching (wherein the horse reflects the nonverbal posture and character of the person) and *systemic* coaching (wherein the horses reflect the systemic environment of the person) can play a role:

- Horse stands at a distance and looks into the distance: the person or the horse wants to get out of the situation.
- Horse is heavy or blocked: the paralyzed feelings of the other horse or man.
- Horse restlessly running around: restlessness in the life of the person or in the environment.

- Horse keeps neck slightly bent: vulnerability of the horse or person.
- Horse nibbling on clothes or body parts: caring, taking care of each other.
- Horse stands on one leg and holds the other loose: relaxation.

In this way, animals know the way to our "heart" and our intuition, and people can be led to more awareness, personal development, and happiness.

A turbulent way to myself, or a traumatic love

❦

DURING MY SYSTEMIC TRAINING, it was also necessary to practice with others and face my own problems. By confronting your own vibrations and issues, you can see the full extent of your personality—from the positive to the negative—and that will give you a broader view and more ability to help others.

For example, during a session, I wondered how I could improve my relationship with my teenage daughter. She often distanced herself from me and only occasionally talked about her feelings and her life, with these instances gradually becoming even more rare. It is an extremely interesting phenomenon, especially in my case, that horses often discover the subject behind the question immediately.

I saw the horses far away from me. The little one that immediately reminded me of my daughter stood on the other side and sometimes looked at me distractedly—it was quite distracted by other people who were outside the field, just like my daughter was preoccupied with her friends. Although this horse was always looking for people's proximity, it actually stood in its role as a distracted and distant child.

The coach asked me for a representative for my daughter, who intuitively turned away from me.

We began to argue, just as I often do with her nowadays, about things like why I was not always there for her. She was angry at me, and I could not fight back. To explain to her the cause of my regular absence seemed too complicated.

There was a certain restless feeling in the air. Clouds moved overhead, and a flock of birds circled over our heads several times. I looked behind me and saw the horse Poppy, another horse, lying on the ground. Apparently, there was something in the earth that pointed to someone who was already in the world of the deceased.

I knew who it was: someone who had given me doubts and had confronted me with my dark side.

The coach appointed another representative for this deceased person. When this representative stood in the middle, he said, "Why can't I rest? Why are you still clinging to something from the past that is connected to me?" I knew that had something to do with my self-love.

I had to complete this chapter, review my beliefs and misunderstandings, take responsibility, find my authentic self, and focus on my own life without the sadness of the past relationship. It touched my heart deeply. Had the relationship influenced me and my decisions so much back then? I took the representative's hands and realized that this had probably happened. The other horses had meanwhile run over to me.

I was able to travel around the world in my job, and I had met a man whom I fell in love with. I could not then see what kind of psychological trap—but at the same time a possibility for further development—this relationship would be.

A person who could say something with complete conviction but act in a different way would probably today be diagnosed with BPD: borderline personality disorder. Since I still had a naïve way of looking at therapeutic cases then, I could not believe that something was wrong and therefore could not monitor enough of my own limits. I even gave up my wonderful job in Burgundy to settle in a cottage in Scotland and start my own business there.

Unfortunately, everything ended with a broken heart; the futile hope that the person would get better was only confirmed in its futility by his suicide. There was, unfortunately, except for my family, little help or understanding from my direct environment. I felt that I had to play the strong person. For months, I thought about what had gone wrong; why had this person been so extreme, and what had been my role in it?

I could not stand the pain and tried to focus on my higher self, which had no limits and would make me feel that there were endless possibilities ahead of me. Reason helped me, to a point. I analyzed typical reactions in such psychological cases and read specialist literature. But true consolation I found more and more through intuition and belief in new possibilities. I felt that I should focus on universal values, such as unconditional love for myself, which gradually gave a place to the events and the person who had "done it" to me.

Being with horses has helped me feel more balanced and restore my self-esteem, along with new activities such as projects in the Middle East, learning new languages and cultures, and last but not least energetic lighting work to recognize and further explore the power of our thoughts and intuition.

My wound would slowly heal as I tried to see the big picture. The wound would sometimes open again at moments when I did not feel understood in my vulnerability; it would affect my digestive system. How had I digested life? In bad moments, I would deal with my first horse, Quieto, and feel recharged afterward. I saw the parallel between the macro and the micro world: as long as there is no proper balance in yourself and you do not fully accept both your sunny and dark sides—this is often the influence of the family, the system—and cannot deliver that love, there will also be no balance in the environment or society in general around you.

This is a universal law that can be applied to all different cultures and—most surprisingly—as I later realized, also to the horse world!

The methodology

MANY COMPANIES WORK WITH a lawyer or quality manager. They distribute questionnaires and have them filled out, hold discussions with employees, and give feedback. Unfortunately, employee appraisals do not yield much because the employees are striving for a certain attitude and often do not feel free enough to say what really matters to them. After all, they are in a delicate position, where management may not get a good picture of them and they may lose their jobs. In addition, such conversations do not really create synergy when employees need to operate in survival mode.

These methods work with role-plays and potential arguments. However, these techniques run on reason and are predominantly verbal, while in fact the unconscious dynamics, patterns of behavior, frustrations, and blockages that run across the emotional world should be addressed within a team.

Here is a reason that coaching with horses is very enlightening: a horse that is instinctively sensitive to its essence, especially when it comes to the survival of the group, shows immediately the tensions, the potential, or the connections, whereas managers need weeks of discussions and evaluations.

Another positive element is that you cannot fool the animals and they are not impressed by status, appearance, or certain masks for survival that help a person feel safer and represent a seemingly strong person. The horse is factually clear, and without judgment it will show the employee or team just what is the most important thing to correct and how to deal with it.

The masks for survival

During childhood, one receives many signals from his or her environment, and the child's parents and must adapt again and again. Every soul has its own way, believe it or not. Every soul, with its individual expectations and events in the background, seeks its place and its self-development in life. Perhaps the first step into life is quite difficult, because of a complicated parenting situation, or very easily because everything has been so well-organized for the child, and the adolescent is given much room to develop.

Depending on the environment, family, or soul path, a child will always receive non verbal messages and signals from its family and other people and must process events and survive at the same time. It wants to be loved and accepted and needs a certain security.

If the young person wishes to protect him- or herself from certain inconvenient events, he or she may eventually use a mask, often one that will be used to protect him or her the rest of his or her life. Until one becomes aware of the limitations of that mask and realizes that it is obstructing open and honest contact, he or she will never have real intimacy or be able to experience a deep connection.

It is fascinating to study these masks. We almost all carry them, some more than others. Everyone will definitely recognize a mask here that applies to him or her and reveals something about a person's character.

Schizoid mask: "The airballoon into the clouds"

THIS PERSON NEEDS THE so-called "travel of the soul" and can completely lose him- or herself in another world. The mental food comes from another world. It just feels good to watch the world from a certain distance, and this knowledge makes sense for your everyday life.

If, for example, a person must remain bedridden for a long time with a plastered leg or is left alone, this character structure can be a way of survival. If you cannot move mentally or physically, the mind gives you the opportunity to do whatever you want.

The biggest need from birth onward is to have the feeling that you can be who you are. If this condition is not there, you will be thrown back on yourself. The only possibility is to flee from loneliness, to take a "air-balloon and disappear into the clouds," so to speak. Contact with others can be difficult, and the only solution is to systemically restore contact with one's absent father and mother and to feel welcome in one's earthly form—in the body—in order to be open to others.

Stephen was a manager. He always had a crystal-clear analysis for his conversations with colleagues. But somehow, one saw and felt that he did not really connect with the others. With the horses, he identified himself most with a horse that stayed at a distance. It stood high on a small hill, static and without movement. The horse showed the typical schizoid mask and somehow seemed to be detached, not really present or in connection with the other horses.

Also, he always kept his distance from the group. When the coach asked him what this reminded him of in the past, he told him that he always had to be the mediator, the conflict-solver, and the intellectual interlocutor of his parents. There was not really any closeness in the family. His mother had never hugged or cuddled him much.

"In fact, my body is not a house address, but rather a holiday address," he said. "I often forget to take a deep breath at work and during stress. I only have regular breathing during outdoor sports." Through this insight, he realized that it was important to have a relationship with his colleagues.

Restoring close or at least some contact with the mother in the systemic field opened new avenues.

With which mask description do you identify most? This little test is just an indication of which mask or mask combination best suits you.

Answer these statements with "yes" or "no":

- "I have trouble with eye contact."
- "I like to retire on my own, and my thoughts are somewhere else, even in conversations."
- "I have retreated from interpersonal contacts."
- "I often have cold hands and feet or stiff joints."
- "I mostly do not feel understood."

Oral mask: The human who never has enough

WHEN A YOUNG PERSON has the impression of giving more than receiving, the feeling of fulfillment and satisfaction disappears. He or she still acts as if he or she gave, but the heart is no longer present. It resists, and the source is often dried up. These feelings are felt by someone with an oral character structure. Somehow the family could not give enough to this person. The child—and the person later as an adult—will always live in the conviction that there is never really enough for him or her.

In a systemic exercise, the coachee was asked to request something he needed from his boss. This caused a great fear in the coachee; he felt blocked asking for it and did not really want to consider his need. "It felt like I was paralyzed or frozen to death, and the request came only partially from myself." There was a lack of conviction, and of course he did not get what he really needed. It created a situation of scarcity, and in this character, for example, a horse would clearly nibble only the barren parts of the grass; the main theme with the horses then seemed to be just eating the food but not being saturated with it.

It takes these people a lot of energy to stay in shape and to feel vitality. This sense of frugality is also felt in relationships, work, and food. You never feel satisfied and fulfilled. Only when you become in tune with yourself and take your real needs seriously can you increase the overall life force in work and private life.

It is good to deal with one's own needs, because it then becomes the task of the adult person to be able to limit and control them.

"Everything in its time" can help as a thought. If you allow this development, a pearl of this character appears: the understanding of what the other needs.

Answer these statements with "yes" or "no":

- "I do not feel welcome on a regular basis."
- "I often wonder in professional or social situations if there is enough left for me."
- "I like to talk about myself."
- "A pleading, questioning look is typical for me."
- "No one is there for me!"

Symbiotic mask

THIS IS THE FEAR of standing alone as an individual; it represents a sense of broken unity, giving one the chance to become an independent individual.

If, as a child, you do not have the opportunity to mentally stand on both your feet and make your own decisions, you will later have problems with autonomy. One seeks only harmony in order not to stand alone, at the expense of one's own individuality and needs and ideas. The task then becomes the ability to learn, to demarcate and stand alone, ultimately discovering one's uniqueness.

This sensitive person can slip into the world and skin of another person incredibly well and lose him- or herself completely. On the other hand, this person can empathize with another so well that if he or she needs to set boundaries, he or she has the feeling of harming the other.

A coachee was standing in the field with the horses, and when she had chosen a place, the horses ran around uneasily and even cut off her way and took her space, so she had to take a step back.

"Can you recognize that in your life?" the coach asked.

"Yes," she said doubtfully. "I find that other colleagues take advantage of me. I always do a lot for them, but I do not really know if it's appreciated."

When the coach asked her to close her eyes and focus on her space and visualize her limits, she calmed down—and the horses again kept a certain distance.

As soon as a person really takes their place in life, or in a company, he or she also dares to deal with others and no longer avoid conflicts. At the same time, he or she can also see what moves the other without being involved.

Answer these statements again with "yes" or "no":

- "I often feel responsible for others and their feelings."
- "In my relationships, I tend to lose myself in the other."
- "I need others to make decisions"
- "When I sit alone in a restaurant, I feel insecure."
- "In discussions, I usually give in."
- "I often do things I do not really want to do."

Rigid mask

HE OR SHE IS always impeccably dressed, has charm, and has good manners. You probably know such a person. However, somehow it is always difficult to establish proper contact with this person, as one often gets stuck in formal utterances or inviting, charming sayings. The person often remains proud and distant in the background for fear of rejection.

The horses see through this mask immediately: they will only feel the underlying feelings and react to them instead.

There was a manager who was a pretty, active woman. She talked a lot, but with the horse in the ring, she suddenly became quiet when she saw how much the horse moved away from her. Her charming behavior obviously made no impression, and the horse seemed more likely to reflect her loneliness, the little girl in her still looking for shelter and security.

In childhood, one becomes aware of one's femininity or masculinity and is pleased to show this. It can be considered as an exercise in the small world. If you do not get the opportunity to experience and deal with it, this emotional development is blocked.

For example, there was a boy who grew up mainly with women. His father was rarely there, and somehow, he could not connect with his male side. He felt uncomfortable with men, missing the example of a male role model; he remained in a kind of intermediate world until his adulthood. The same applies to girls.

These people are not yet able to connect properly with their appropriate femininity or masculinity. They cannot somehow show their vulnerability and do not indulge with others, fearing not being fully accepted.

Answer these statements with "yes" or "no":

- "I find it hard to show my sensitive side."
- "I never want to lose control."
- "I need some emotional distance from my partner."
- "I prefer to do my job perfectly."
- "I have a tilted back pelvis."
- "I tend to stand with an inflated chest".

Psychopathic mask

THIS TYPE OF PERSON uses distrust as protection in the struggle for survival, relying only on themselves; only the performance is important, and it leads to losing connections.

Here we see the child who felt left alone and who wants to solve everything in life. He or she was hurt in his or her confidence in early childhood and now prefers to do everything without "the others."

For example, something in a boy's childhood left him very disappointed; his parents may have left him alone with an important problem. Maybe the situation in the family was sometimes difficult and the boy had to learn very early to solve everything alone; but this has also left wounds, apart from an independent attitude. He often distances himself from others and provides harsh criticism. He has difficulty with a deeper emotional connection. As a result, a mentality develops in his life that he is convinced of the power of the strongest. He will set the conditions by assuming a lack of trust and leave little room for the other.

In coaching, he should learn, for his own balance, how much power is in vulnerability and how he really makes deeper connections with himself, other people can enter.

The person will show himself bigger and stronger than he really is: "Let me do that"; "No one can rely on others"; and "Alone I can still do it best" will be much-heard statements.

The horse stood beside the self-confident man and made himself taller than the man. He stretched his head and put it on the man's as if to make him smaller.

Answer these statements with "yes" or "no":

- "I want to win."
- "I often go beyond my own limits."
- "I distrust other people."
- "I often stand with my wide feet apart."
- "If I break a friendship, it will be forever."

Masochistic mask

A HUMAN BEING WITH this mask always has the feeling of being under pressure and having to do much more. Under this mask, he or she is particularly concerned with the fate of other people but unfortunately does not come to what he or she likes to do him- or herself. The choice is either to "express" and "create expression and space" for oneself or "depression."

In childhood, a man often knew compulsion and only had little opportunity to express his feelings. Being able to bear his own feelings was the sign of his independence. But this was also mixed with feelings of revenge and passive aggression and inner anger.

When in a coaching session, he should learn to express his own will and acceptance of his boundaries to help others.

During a coaching session, the coachee stood in front of his parents. He wanted to go or run away to lead his own life. His father seemed to tell him to "just go." However, his mother's eyes told him clearly, "Please stay. I have it so hard." The horse beside the person, who was clearly representing his mother, stood heavy and unstable on its legs.

The coachee decided: he gave his mother a symbolic burden and turned away to live his own life. As a child, he was feeling "angry and sad" and felt running away was the only way, and at the same time, he felt guilty that he had betrayed her to create a space for himself.

The only solution to this character structure is to limit suffering and guilt and to allow for life and also joy and lightness. This session was all about the son and his development, his need to rid himself of the masochistic attitude to live in freedom. After the session, both persons representing his parents, and feeling their emotions, responded positively to the independent attitude of the son. They had now experienced and truly felt with the body that it was their burden the son had carried: the father's expectations, with a rather rigid character structure that followed his principles, and the mother's anxiety, with a typical oral structure causing her to be left behind or remain unloved. These unspoken feelings blocked the young man, and the parents could finally see this because they felt it on an emotional level. You really only love others when you give them freedom and allow them to take responsibility for their own feelings; then everyone finds their own balance between give and take.

The mood, energy, and relationship between the family members had changed noticeably. The young man could breathe deeply after the spoken words; they changed the dynamics, despite the fact that his parents had not been present physically.

However, the client is advised not to talk too much at the end of a session or to follow up on details with the mind. In this way, the feeling and insights can integrate better with all involved.

Answer these statements with "yes" or "no":

- "I find it hard to say no."
- "I like helping others, but I often feel exploited."
- "I have problems with digestion."
- "I tend toward depression."
- "I like to listen to the other person; I have a lot of patience."

The paths to harmony

"I WILL LEAVE YOU! I feel a total loneliness in our relationship!" yelled Stephen's wife, Cybil, uncontrollably.

Stephen had approached his wife after his walk and had tried to approach her with a hug. She pushed him away and reacted in a very reserved manner. "What exactly is the matter?" he asked her. But then only allegations were made.

"I do not know if I want to continue," she said after she had stopped yelling.

"Well, let's do some marriage counselling," Stephen replied. "Maybe there are still some solutions; we do not want to give up everything right away."

One day, the two were in a horse arena, just to try it out, as their therapist had said, "We have already had a long conversation and discussions. Is it not about time to give the unconscious its place, the systemic order, and to stay outside the words?" Stephen and Cybil were tired after all the dialogues and allegations. One could indeed sink into words, reproaches, and theories. But what about their love, their feelings, and the unconscious patterns they carried with them? However, they were somewhat reserved: systemic coaching with horses? Did that make sense? But then, why not give something new a chance?

The horses stayed away from the couple after the wife took a seat. Cybil was the main questioner and had to relax first with some breathing exercises to turn off her circular thoughts. After that, she went intuitively to a place in the ring, following her gut feeling.

The mare halted in the arena; the other horses stayed outside the stables. The coach asked her if she recognized something in the scene. Cybil recognized something: she identified herself with the mare, loyal and a bit anxious in the arena. The mare stood as motionless as if she had been paralyzed by something and looked at the other horses.

"How would you describe the mare? And why are you paralyzed?" the coach asked.

"I actually feel a lack of energy, and I keep asking myself if the kids are doing well and looking after my husband, but he's almost gone."

"Which of the horses would you identify as your husband, and which as your children?"

Intuitively, Cybil knew that the two horses looking into the distance were their children; they stood a little farther away and had begun to move, meanwhile. She "saw" her husband in a different horse standing on the other side, a little separated; the man in person had intuitively added himself.

The coach asked her which horses she felt most attracted to and whether she could go there. She ran to the horses that represented her children. The moment she walked to them, the horses moved a little farther away, totally focused on other things. This happened again and again as Cybil began to move and attempted to seek contact with the horses.

"What do you feel because of that?" the coach asked. She became thoughtful and looked a bit perplexed.

It felt like she was getting in the way of them or somehow as if she would hassle them. "I'm always a bit worried. In fact, my daughter often tells me to give her a little more room to do her things."

"Oh!" Cybil said suddenly, "I think they are very happy, and without any worries, they are able to follow their life."

"And what about your own life?" the coach asked. She was very quiet and had to admit that, in fact, she did not have one.

"I'm not sure where I belong anymore," she said.

Cybil saw that the horse representing her husband was still standing motionless beside the stables.

"He's also like that horse, totally absorbed in other things, just not the kids or me. I think he's going to have a burnout, the way he lives," she said, a bit bitterly.

The coach suggested that her own heart should be represented. There were a few people who were invited as representatives, and she was allowed to choose one from them. Nature was quiet again, and the mare, which represented Cybil, suddenly moved to one of the women present and stopped there.

"That's weird," Cybil said. "I was just about to ask her."

The woman, who now represented her heart, walked into the field and stopped far away from Cybil.

"Why do you want to stand here, heart of Cybil?" asked the coach.

"I cannot go on," she said. "I have to keep my distance, away from her."

"Does that tell you something?" the coach ask ed Cybil.

"Yes, I cannot get in touch with what I really, profoundly want. I'm alien to myself." She cried and stood, a bit lost, in the middle.

51

"Could you walk to your heart and make a new contact with it?"

It was fascinating how much this representative could feel the energy and emotions of the heart, even if she did not know the person at all. This is the deep body-knowledge, the sensitivity to energy, the intuition that all of us carry within ourselves.

Tears streamed down her cheeks as Cybil looked into the eyes of her heart and they held hands. She had the feeling of finding herself again. The mare came and tenderly put her nose on both hands to seal that energy.

The right words are important and provide a whole new energy and dynamism that influence a person's system and behavior:

"I am your heart, and I only beat for you; never let go of me, and listen to me."

"You are my heart, and you are just beating for me; I will always carry you and be with you."

By now, the mare was standing motionless by her and her "heart" and in between her and her husband. Then, the very moment she made contact with her heart, the other "children" horses came closer to her again, which she immediately noticed.

When she turned her attention from her heart to her husband, the mare moved to the side and opened the way to her husband.

As they walked towards each other, the energy was very different. Since Cybil had taken the first step to owning her own power and potential, to her heart, and was able to let go—in this case, of her worries about her children—her husband could also feel freer to develop his authentic power and establish a new relationship.

As they faced each other, they both felt a new love that could evolve. It was not yet the end of this journey together to solve their common problems, but the first step, the first inner movement of feeling and unconsciousness, had been made, at least.

Three horses had lined up around the couple in the foal position, as if to protect this private, tender, vulnerable moment from the eyes of others. The moment was magical and demonstrated the tremendous power of the heart the horses can impart, revealing their talents as therapists who want to help people in the present and without any judgment.

We carry such an experience with us for a long time, and we need some time to digest and fathom for ourselves the impact of it.

Germany

Every human being is shaped by a culture and its language. There are certain concepts in each culture and language that you cannot necessarily find in another culture. Certain words or expressions cannot be directly translated into another language, so there is simply not always an adequate translation that equally reflects the content.

Germany's culture consists of many aspects of very divers regions and historical backgrounds, but compared to other European countries, there is a general tendency in society toward its own codes and contexts.

In international business, one often uses the stereotype of the pragmatic German approach, always having a purpose, with appropriate courtesy, a society with a predefined hierarchy and the need for and usage of the proper titles; it is a society in which logic dominates and one likes to control situations and systems. This may have been a consequence of the postwar period, during which creating, planning, and organizing provided a sense of security; a traumatic experience will leave a systemic mark on both a person and a society. Reliability is the key word in many walks of German life.

The quality and credibility of the contact always comes first; one wants to be taken seriously and get into business pretty quickly. "They [Germans] are so serious," a French colleague once said to me, "that you should not joke at the first business meeting."

In German business, establishing good contacts is just as important as in other countries, but there is a clear separation between home and office. This is something that is not so consistently separated in Italy, for example, or Spain; personal contact in the private sphere is also the basis for long-term business in those places.

Although there is a certain work ethic in Germany and Germans abroad are portrayed as very diligent, there is a term they use that one does not find in other cultures: *Feierabend,* which literally means "celebration-evening," referring to closing time. If you call a German office a few minutes after five, you often do not reach anyone—a rarity in other countries.

An evening without really doing anything is taken seriously. This is one of the historical achievements of Germany in their work approach and is certainly also a reason why their society has developed economically so well. In other languages and cultures, one would call it, as the historian Wilhelm Heinrich Riehl described, in his best known work is *Die Naturgeschichte des deutschen Volkes als Grundlage einer deutschen Socialpolitik,* 4 vol. (1851–69; "The Natural History of the German People as a Foundation of German Social Politics"), in which he emphasized geographical factors, social conditions, and German local life and culture: an "an atmosphere of carefree wellbeing, of deep inner reconciliation, of the pure and clear quiet of the evening". (translated by The Guardian: https://www.theguardian. com/world/2018/jul/27/10-of-the-best-words-in-the-world-that-dont-translate-into-english).

It is a concept that does not seem so obvious elsewhere.

For the function of a manager, a good education, experience, and commitment are required in terms of qualifications.

Unfortunately, emotional intelligence is often ignored because it is not developed, tested, and promoted in the various training programs as such.

For example, many managers focus on efficiency and innovation in technical and logistical processes, on the so-called process tweaking, but empathetic communication directly with their employees does not exist. In many teams, there is hidden tension, frustration, and even bullying of employees. All this may lead to increasing burnout problems and absenteeism among workers.

Again, the role of executives in such cases is often responsible for this. They have no real, purely human interest in their own employees, are unable to listen to them because they lack openness and commitment in their own communication, do not demand or promote adequately, give little constructive and fair feedback, and give hardly any active support or recognition in their output; they avoid conflicts and do not create a "we/us feeling." The list of such behaviors could be continued. Employee surveys can show such problems.

Also, among the teams, emotional intelligence, self-responsibility, and the consideration of their personal and possibly systemic background, as well as the unconscious behavior patterns, are also extremely important for the employees themselves. Unfortunately, they, too, are not always particularly eager to deal with their superiors. From my experiences in business life, they are often upset, but they do not always take the responsibility to resolve an unclear situation or conflict. Needless to say, a balance in giving and taking is important in every environment.

How, then, can managers prevent such failures? Emotional intelligence helps enormously. The American psychologist Daniel

Goleman developed this term in the mid-1990s. Meanwhile, there are numerous studies that show that managers with a strong EQ are more successful than those who rely solely on their IQ. Emotional intelligence consists of three elements:

1. Self-reflection: the ability to realistically assess one's own strengths and weaknesses, needs, and values. Managers with good self-reflection are looking for constructive feedback from others—also and especially from their fellow colleagues. They are honest with themselves and do not have to fool others.

2. Self-management: the ability not to become a prisoner of one's own feelings and also remain constructive in cases of frustration or anger. Studies show that executives who are often in a good mood are more productive than others.

3. Motivation: managers with high motivation place high demands, first of all on themselves, and then on their teams. They develop a true dedication to what they do, and they remain confident in times of great challenges.

Recently, a German scientist complained about the "zombies" in many companies: employees who simply no longer feel enthusiastic about their work. One often feels trapped and slowed down with initiatives because there is no time for dialogue, and no room for it: "Time is money—next, please!"

Today, the best example of this is probably a call center, which measures exactly how many customers you helped and for how many minutes; even the time for a toilet visit is being monitored.

Are not these social "zombies" ultimately a consequence of politics, where "sustainability" and "respect for humans" are only slogans without content? Such a policy is taken for granted when the exploitation of people, countries, and their natural resources through outsourcing is considered normal. Many companies that have lost their soul, the enthusiasm of the team and the individual employee, due to a policy of greed, where money is not a means to add value in life but the goal itself in trade and society.

It is really time to adopt a new philosophy, one that finally realizes that everything and all countries are linked with each other and that together we are responsible for a better society.

And of course, we all know of so-called evaluation interviews, which in professional life hang like a dark cloud over the heads of every employee. It is the moment when everyone is judged by a questionnaire, and any possible complaint, "hearsay," or new demands are being expressed. Based on the questionnaires, everything is then somehow measured, sometimes without substantiated further essential knowledge about the person and his or her motivations. Here, unfortunately, the question of the motives of action, as well as the dialogue about it, comes too short.

It's a race where you try to appear in the best possible light and ethical behavior is not necessarily a priority.

Not everything is as it seems

HORSE-ASSISTED COACHING REQUIRES NO experience in dealing with horses. You will not have to ride or even sit on a horse, and you will also have enough time for detailed instruction in handling the animals. If you are really afraid of horses, you will be gently brought into gradual contact with the horses.

The goal of coaching

Horses are excellent feedback providers. In dealing with them, one recognizes and experiences his or her individual behavior and communication patterns very intensively. In the coaching process, we will question these patterns, try out alternative approaches, and together develop a personal target image and a concrete implementation plan. In this way, we can successively consolidate the transfer of findings in everyday life.

The participants recognize their potential for development and change, and they learn to make their communication clearer and more human.

Some sales managers came to me one day for equine-assisted leadership coaching. The director, who had organized this workshop with me, also found it interesting and wanted to be there. The group consisted mainly of men, with only two women participating. They made mischievous jokes and laughed a lot, probably to lessen the tension in the—as yet—unknown coaching method. The director remained fairly formal, showing his authority and respectful presence. He seemed to be someone who could express himself powerfully and had everything under control.

The meeting point was a ranch in Münsterland, Germany. Fortunately, all was very tranquil, and we could calmly focus on the coaching of each individual manager. This time, we would do an intrapersonal, reflective session with each participant to analyze their respective leadership styles and nonverbal communication and further optimize it with the help of the horses and do an exercise. This exercise would certainly bring out unconscious patterns of behavior, something that could be quite confrontational. For this purpose, we used a small ring with a horse that could move freely, and with its body-language, it reflected the behavior of the manager.

The director gladly presented himself as the first guinea pig. I asked him to do some breathing exercises first and relax. The advantage of this is that a person totally focuses on him- or herself, becomes aware of his or her feelings and body, and thus senses his or her intuition. As coaches, we ask people to always rely on their physical feelings and to go where their legs are carrying them. Confident and controlled, the man in the arena took a position as if he wanted to start a business meeting.

Horses are not impressed by titles, functions, or appearance and instead immediately react to the essence of a person. The man did not stand far from the horse. At that moment, the horse walked slightly toward him and seemed to make itself taller than the man. The man straightened himself, as if trying to elongate himself in order to show the horse his authority and control. After a few seconds, the horse took a confronting stance and even slightly pushed its head against his shoulder and arm.

I asked him what he felt. He responded that he felt like he was in a conflict. When I asked him if he recognized this situation in his professional life, he admitted that he often had arguments with colleagues; this was because of protocols and deadlines that needed to be met. Of course, one should be productive at work, but was the communication appropriate?

He had to think for a moment and did not immediately come up with an answer. He was obviously quite taken aback by the experience with the horse.

I asked the man to close his eyes and relax a little more—the tension around him could be felt—and to focus on his breath and the feeling. In the moment when someone establishes a connection between mind and feeling and relaxes, a completely different energy arises. After a few moments, the horse relaxed more and stood a bit more calmly next to him. It was an exercise this person also could do during work.

Here, one deals with a conditioning, an unconscious behavior that has been defined by our education and environment, in order to have everything under control and to perform a function as perfectly as possible. This in itself causes a certain amount of stress, with many people unconsciously believing that something is never good enough. Such people could quickly move into burnout. This happens when you believe your own natural person is not enough and should be constantly perfected.

However, proper leadership is about increasing autonomy and letting go rather than holding the strings in your hands.

When the man wanted to get out of the ring, the horse played with the headcollar that was lying on the ground. This play and touch of bridle or halter is indeed interpreted as conditioning of the human being. When I asked the manager, he was surprised and did not seem to have considered this option yet. Almost every person is more or less conditioned and influenced by his personal, unconscious beliefs, as well as injuries from the past. There is then a tendency to adapt to the expectations of others. The m anager's seemingly strong attitude in this case was a mask around this conditioning to mask his weaknesses.

In systemic coaching with horses, you could go even deeper into the subject and clarify and correct the influence of parents or other family members during early childhood.

In the systemic realm, it is ultimately about this balance between giving and receiving. If humans still carry this influence and all that they have heard from their parents, they can never really live life in freedom. Especially in a manager job, you feel the benefit if you are not blocked by restricting unconscious beliefs in your contact with the team.

The next manager was a very quiet, even a shy person; he said little in the group.

As he stood in the arena, the same horse stood quite calmly and relaxed beside him. When the man started to walk, the horse followed him; when he stopped, the horse behind him stood still too. An unbelievable chemistry became visible, and there were natural leadership qualities revealed in this manager that one would not have guessed. "In calm, there is strength," our family used to say. Just to find oneself in oneself, to remain authentic, simply to *be* in the present and not to need a "ruler type" attitude, enables one to better master situations and gain more connection with other people.

It showed a personality to which human resource managers and sales directors mostly would not react positively. They often fall for the bravery-facade, outward appearances that often obscure uncertainty and seem rather intimidating to many people, as implicitly it is indeed intended to intimidate others.

That's why I believe that it really is time to change the belief system in the field of personnel and recruitment and time to demand more knowledge, empathy, and vision. Only then can you start sustainable companies in which people feel comfortable!

A team: Process tweaking or human potential?

IT REMAINS A VERY current issue for sustainable companies nowadays: how can we optimize processes and teams? It is well known that human potential is often more decisive in success than continuous process tweaking. But what are then the prerequisites for optimal conditions? And how do you perform a holistic, balanced leadership?

Unfortunately, it is not enough just to look at the individual employee; you must see the dynamics of a whole team. Often there are hidden tensions, frustration, or many unspoken things, apart from a lack of communication, that make it impossible to work together optimally. The consequences are thus increasing absences for sick leave and burnout problems, therefore creating extra pressure on the team because someone else has to do the work. That is not cost-saving. Unfortunately, this will then also be costly for the manager and the CEO—not to mention the extra stress.

In such a case, we deal with a lack of synergy and trust among colleagues. It should not be forgotten that the management style plays an important role here: is one-sided communication predominant among managers, or is communication between all colleagues flowing? And here again, the emotional intelligence of the manager plays an important role.

But also, the "system" of each person plays in this context a not-to-be underestimated role and determines the chemistry within the team. Does everyone take their place, their position? Or are there any obstacles there—whether hidden or not? Does everyone in this system—the team or company—feel valued so that they can use their full potential and connect with others?

You will certainly be confronted with these questions more often in the future, precisely because you want to become (and remain) a sustainably optimized company.

One such team consisted of ten therapists and social workers who frequently had to work together. Each therapist was responsible for a specific neighborhood in the city. Communication was still essential, even though they mostly had contact over the phone and email and only met incidentally.

I asked the members of the group to each choose a place in the arena. They each took their position—quite far apart from each other; a certain distance could be felt. Everyone had a place in their (professional) field, of course, but you should also be able to take your own place. The horses stayed on the side for the time being and did not seek any contact. They enjoyed themselves with small leaves on the willow tree next to them and had no eye for the people or the beautiful, good, fresh grass in other places. The horses showed little desire for contact and indicated a certain lack, or need, symbolized by the nibbling of the willow leaves. A vital question in systemic work, which should always be pursued in order to stay on the right track, is, "How is the atmosphere, and how is the contact in the group?"

The team reacted in a reserved manner. One person started talking about the protocols at work. Others talked about the daily pressure. At that moment, a horse ran into the group from the outside and stopped near a person in the middle.

I asked the woman what she thought the horse wanted to tell her. It remained silent, and the woman did not immediately speak, but then she said that everyone on the team only worked for themselves. Then the group went fully silent again.

The horse suddenly placed itself next to the woman, between her and me (in the foal position). There was a small sob: the woman began to tell how she had been fighting burnout for some time, and no one had ever been interested in her situation; others would constantly talk about protocols and exert even more pressure. The group was silent, and when I asked if anyone knew about it, the dialogue slowly started.

After that, the horse walked to another person, an employee who had a lot to do with the first person, as it turned out. She began to apologize and said she had not realized how lonely the woman had felt at work ... their feelings were almost never talked about at work.

The group came closer to each other, and they stood together in a circle at a certain point. The horses had opened up new opportunities for cooperation through mutual dialogue.

Although business life in Germany is rather rigid regarding emotions in the work environment, this new experience in nature was perceived as very positive and authentic.

France

AT A RANCH IN Gruissan in the south of France, I worked with four horses: Quieto, Juan, Olaf, and Querido, along with more horses standing around them on an open, stable terrain. To correctly explain the idea of systemic work with the aid of horses was quite difficult from the very start—and it still is. The activity is easily confused with "horse whispering" or compared to other vague New Age phenomena that are difficult to understand. There seems to be an aspect of threat to people in working on personal development because it exposes them to weaknesses or uncertainties.

The term "emotional intelligence" is often viewed with skepticism by French scientists, probably because France is a very reason-oriented society in which certain traditions, bureaucracy, hierarchies, and protocols are still considered very important. Add to this the fact that the concept of systemic coaching comes from the United States and Anglo-Saxon culture; it is therefore often not considered a positive thing in France, because it is too little concerned with their cultural differences, especially in recent years, and thus represents a kind of "winning culture" without ethics in business.

"Americans just do too much," is a feeling many French have. The French live more "right now," to appreciate the moment at the table with family and friends on the terrace. The "excited" emotions of Anglo-Saxon cultures, for example, are lesser known in France.

"Emotions stand in the way of career opportunities," says French journalist Jean Laurent Casseley. "When analyzing data or repairing cars as a job, it can be extremely impractical to have to read the facial expressions, postures of people around you. In such jobs, emotional intelligence makes less sense." (translation by author)

Alas, the author in his somewhat archaic view forgets that a service provider must establish good contact with its customers in order to keep them as clients. Emotions, of course, should be authentic, but a supplier who cannot listen and respond to the needs of his or her clients has only limited control over his or her business. In addition, a good deal of empathy could also enrich his or her private life.

Unfortunately, it is also thought that emotional intelligence could be used for manipulative purposes. In fact, highly intelligent people can indeed influence others in this way. But the emotional intelligence that exists in horses—and that should actually only bear this name—is the inner intuitive knowledge and feeling that we are all connected and at the same time serve a larger whole. This is what is meant by "a person standing in his or her own authentic power," whereby it is not necessary to compensate for frustration or selfishness through manipulation. Horses will not know these psychopathic masks and will thus instantly show people their masks in a session and reveal the systemic reason why these masks are worn. Above all, emotional intelligence should establish a better relationship with oneself and others and create more harmony in the environment!

Regrettably, the concept of this intelligence is too often used for neoliberal purposes, and sustainability and ethics are then neglected.

The French opponents of the need for emotional intelligence, however, offer no alternative to promote humanity and sustainability in the economy. In politics and the economy, the development of personal, emotional abilities is considered meaningful only when seen by the board or the elite, which is not usually the case in French culture. This makes communication at eye level in many areas more difficult, and frustrations remain hidden until the negative energy becomes too much and the whole matter actively explodes in passive aggression or, ultimately, a conflict in society, such as a revolt or revolution.

The Frenchman is educated in his school system with Cartesian principles, which are conservative and thus based on many old ideas. Conservative institutions guard over sufficient input of French culture and language—unfortunately neglecting the optimization of foreign languages and language lessons; young people are not thrilled with old-fashioned topics and boring texts on the grammar of foreign languages.

Mathematics and philosophy can be wonderful subjects, but there is a lack of refreshing ideas and approaches.

In addition, the promotion of empathic skills is fully in the background. The French student should only do something according to the old set model and criteria.

For example, if someone in school experiences dyslexia or high sensitivity and receives poor grades, he or she will fail in the world outside of the school system, or at least face prejudice from society. Unfortunately, this is a phenomenon that exists in other countries, too, and it takes away the pleasure in learning. What is the purpose of learning if the heart, feeling, or enthusiasm is not there?

Studies have proven time and again that in such circumstances, you absorb less and remember the substance only for a short time.

Nonetheless, the path to the future remains mostly conventional, and most companies also view training and education as something that is useful only in certain limited cases. Personality development is certainly not considered a priority.

According to an article of Dilip Subramanian and Bénédicte Zimmermann on corporate and individual training of employees in France, we read the following:

> The article discusses the impact of organizational configurations on employees' training capabilities. Inspired by the capability approach, it uses qualitative data to question under what organizational conditions firms in France provide their employees with the opportunities and means to participate not just in training programmes, but in those programmes they have reason to value. The results suggest the existence of three different training models—skill-updating, skill-developing and capability-enhancing—depending on the choice processes involved, the importance they accord to employee agency, and the training outcomes. While human resource policies offering training opportunities are important in French organizations, enabling individual capability ultimately depends on employee participation schemes. The article further argues that this goal cannot be achieved through collective voice alone; in vocational training, individual voice plays an equally central role.

The Languedoc area is an extreme example of this trend. The people in this region are very traditional and have to be guided by certain conventions and common ideas. This area was still economically isolated twenty years ago. Unlike with its neighboring Côte d'Azur, it was not until the 1990s that tourism was promoted and developed through the development of new projects, new investors, and other economic activities in the Languedoc region. Nevertheless, most people have always lived in the same area. If they are ill, they will visit a doctor; if they feel depressed, they will go to a psychologist. Other related professions do not have a very stable status, because people do not have much experience with alternative therapy and coaching options.

The perception of horses in France is, above all, a traditional one: man controls the horses—his possession—and uses them for work, riding, or for sport. The horse should obey its owner. Although the idea of a partnership between man and horse is slowly being introduced, the horse is not yet recognized as a master for coaching purposes!

Coaching with horses is not a common phenomenon in France. There are workshops à la Rupert Isaacson in some equestrian facilities, and there are a few coaches who specialize in reflective coaching in France, but participation (e.g., from companies) is still very limited. This should definitely be further developed!

Success in professional life:
The question behind
the question

"I'M NOT SURE WHAT I want to know about," she said uncertainly on the phone. "Maybe more success in my professional life would be interesting. I have tried to get through it everywhere without success!"

Valérie had contacted me on Facebook and wanted to try this new kind of coaching. I felt like she was looking at it as just a game, because she asked me what kind of dressage figures she had to ride.

I explained to her that one would only work with the nature of the horses and discuss life issues through their systemic sensitivity.

Since this type of coaching was not known in the region, I just wanted to offer it to local residents. A few acquaintances had reacted anxiously and answered, "No, I feel good, all right!" or, "I'm a bit skeptical of horse whisperers."

Of course, I then had to explain further and mention that horse whisperers do something completely different and that this coaching is not about magic or esoteric ideas but about completely natural logic.

And so, on a Saturday, Valérie stood in front of me with her husband and children. I asked her if she wanted her husband to participate in the coaching. "Yes, of course!" she answered.

It's fascinating how "coincidence" brings together the people and issues needed to help clients. Valérie had a question about her professional life, and she certainly thought she was protected from deeper issues.

The horse, however, is extremely honest in its nature and will produce just what is essential for the development of a human, an element he or she can continue to be working on further.

Valérie had horses of her own and felt equally comfortable between Quieto, Juan, Olaf, Tanka, and Querido. I explained to her again how the coaching is conducted and that she herself must follow her own feelings. The moment I asked a question or suggested something, I would always see if that was really true for her.

Valérie picked a spot in the field, between the horses, where she felt comfortable at the moment. All the horses were walking around restlessly, as if there was no proper balance in the area.

I asked her if she recognized something in their uneasiness around her and what she believed about where this might come from. She replied that she did indeed feel a great deal of stress in her work.

"And in your private life?" I asked.

"Yes," she admitted, "there too!"

The horse Quieto had stood at some distance from the others and stood there very calmly, in contrast to the rest. "Who could that be?" I asked her.

Without pause, she said impulsively, "This is my husband. He always stays calm! Everyone will ask him for advice."

Her husband was now out of the field, distracted by other things. I asked Valérie if she would like to get closer to her husband. But she did not have that feeling; somehow it became clear that she needed distance.

I asked the husband to take a place in the field, and without having heard our conversation, he moved farther away from her, near Quieto, with whom he unconsciously identified himself.

I showed Valérie the distance. She shrugged her shoulders and said that was the way it had always been. Her face looked sad and a bit confused. She did not seem to expect that, and it went deeper than she thought.

Tanka was also very far away from her. Whom did he represent? Someone else who was aloof from her in the family? Far away in a corner?

"My father!" she said impulsively. Then she paused, as if she had said too much. The natural environment and the horses made her more open than she normally was.

Quite naturally, the conversation suddenly shifted to her mother, who had been separated from her father for years. She had a good relationship with her mother, although the contact was always very hectic and the mother was often critical of her. She clearly saw the mother figure in the presence of Juan, who was grazing not far away. I asked her to give the place of her mother to a representative (someone had volunteered for it).

When I asked about her father, she was a bit reserved. "I do not want to talk about him. He somehow disappeared when I was young, and he has been recently trying to contact me, but I do not want that.."

I felt there were a lot of unprocessed emotions here and we should focus on her mother first. The mother was quite aloof—the representatives somehow automatically show the attitude of the person they represent and feel the energy and their thoughts and feelings, at least partially or even more.

"She was never warm to me!" Valérie said. "But since I have my daughter and she regularly babysits her when I work, we talk a bit more with each other."

At that moment, Querido, the younger horse, came forward and stood between mother and daughter, gently placing his nose on both hands as they looked at each other.

The words of love came clumsily out of the mother's mouth.

"Just like my mother; she cannot express her feelings," said Valérie.

But with the daughter, it became easier for her. Her biological daughter was also playful. Tears came to Valérie's eyes, and she said she understood her mother better now: she knew that she did not have much love from her own parents. The daughter would now have created a new opening between the two. Querido stood tenderly between the two and clearly embodied the daughter.

Valérie sighed and saw this as the end of the session. "I feel emotionally stronger this way."

She wanted to get away and thank the other horses, as one usually does with such coaching. Then she wanted to approach her husband, who was even farther away, alone in the field.

But when Valérie approached her husband, her path was blocked by Olaf, the Frisian. He refused to move aside and was very clear in his signal: she should approach Tanka, her father!

I felt it very clearly and asked Valérie what she felt.

"He's pushing me toward Tanka!"

"Why do you think he does that?" I asked.

"This is my dad, but I do not want to have anything to do with him."

"Olaf seems to find it important to do something there for the sake of your own happiness and development."

"I do not want to," she reiterated adamantly.

I would have pushed such a person, trying to convince her. Somehow this father embodied me; sometimes my daughter would avoid me just the same way, and was that fair? But in the past, I had also felt responsible for making unhappy people happy again.

The decision to be happy can only come from the person. No one but that person can force him or her to do so. I had a whole love story based on this "saving" complex, and now I finally had the feeling for myself to take responsibility for my own happiness. Helping others is done best by simply being a witness and holding space for them, supporting them, and facilitating the process.

So I took my place and stood beside the woman as an empathic observer and partner.

"It's fine," I said. "Let it work quietly within you; digest all this. It was quite a big step already. You can always come back."

"Yes, of course," she said, feeling glad that she was freed.

Only in freedom can you make your choice and make important decisions.

"It was very intense," she said. "I'd like to come back to it, maybe in a while."

The assertive and empathic sides of a person are influenced by his or her parents in the first years. Does the child get space and trust to develop? Does the father, or a male confidant, give the son the power to assert himself and have enough self-confidence? Is the mother perhaps very distracted with her attention and does not confirm enough the female side of the daughter?

Somehow, the horses in this session showed that the coachee had lacked male attention; the assertiveness was not completely worked out. The connection with the male personality part should be restored by reconciling with her father, accept the total package of his personality, and thus also with her partner, with whom there was an obvious distance.

This situation certainly also has an impact in working life; the pattern of behavior continues and is not newly addressed internally. Horses go straight to the essence of a topic, and that was clearly the case with this session.

Olaf did not even want to let the client go without her having made peace with this part of her, making it "whole" again.

But a person's own will has the last word.

"First love" in a session with a French couple

A COUPLE FROM THE region arranged a coaching appointment with me. The lady had a question about her relationship. She mentioned that she often felt that her partner was pretty cold toward her. The horses Olaf and Querido walked straight to her and showed her easy access to their emotional world, but Juan and Quieto stayed away. She recognized her mother in Juan, who remained emotionally distant from her and did not want to show her appreciation. But had she herself shown esteem to her mother? She looked at her mother's representative and began to cry, saying, "I regret not having appreciated her enough."

At that moment, there was suddenly an unplanned disturbance from an unexpected corner; somewhere on the ranch, a man began yelling, and the lady said without looking, "That is like my ex. He was very dominant and always screamed at me the same way!" The horses were chased out of the field by the unrest, and only Querido and Juan stayed with the woman. With a representative for her ex-husband, she was able to complete this story and return the burden she bore for him. After this intervention, Juan opened the door to her husband, and Querido stood between the two and me to give the couple that private moment.

In this session, first love was not mentioned initially but brought in by the unexpected "representative" who at that moment represented part of their system. The problem between the woman and this man had to be treated first. It should be felt anew, to be suffered again. She could express her gratitude for their time together and give him back what was not hers and let him go.

The man did not want to take his own burden, yet when the lady realized how much power she had, she did not feel dependent on his approval and even felt relieved. I explained to the lady that the screaming man at the ranch was part of the system at that moment and absolutely important to her spiritual personal development and her relationship with her current husband.

Italy

IT WOULD BE SAID that Italy is the land of the sun, culture, and emotions. But of course, there are also conventions that are often still very influenced by the Catholic Church and eventual misinterpretations: the acceptance of patriarchal structures, where the father in a family has the last word and sons are pampered by their mothers, especially in the South of the country; the glorification of a mother figure in society, an idea associated with the holy Mary, Here, the expression of emotions is part of the culture, but also the outward appearance—*la bella figura*—the elegance of presentation, and the first impression play an incredibly important role. If you succeed in doing so; like presenting yourself with elegant clothes, an interesting appearance and cultivate a culture of flattering or complimenting other people, and play the role of the ancient Roman emperors, you can often live a long life in a career without really doing anything concrete for it!

In Italy we see new developments in the economy and society in which young people feel alone, are not accepted by the outside world, and do not sufficiently deal with their emotional world. There are signs of growing emotional distress, especially among children and young people. Along with this atmosphere comes the social crisis. What is particularly striking is the increase in violence among young people. Italy has the highest murder rate in the world, after the United States. This shows that some Italian minors have serious deficiencies in self-control, an inability to cope with their anger, and a lack of empathy. On the possibility for developing social and emotional intelligence, communications expert Marc A. Pletzer notices that companies in Germany use rather the anonymization, in order to be able to lead the customer more easily into a condition of the purchase frenzy. Here social contacts would only distract. This, perhaps that the marketplace or supermarket maybe lost their function as a meeting-place. The question remains, where will people meet in a few years for such an exchange? If you visit southern countries like Italy, then you will be able to observe this kind of exchange between people, especially in smaller communities, in the evening. Of course, these are also very good places to train social skills, togetherness. Especially in Germany, these forums seem to be lost, and the lack of contacts is compounded by massive television consumption, ubiquitous computer games and gambling dens. The church has also lost this function for many in the past ten to fifteen years, and so far, it seems nothing equivalent to replace such. The ability to live alone does not mean that every member of a society must actually make use of this opportunity. He notes that it may be much more meaningful, especially since the increasing loneliness of many people, to specifically train social skills

The loneliness of man in society certainly has to do with the lack of these social meeting places and abilities. Social media has replaced the marketplace and the church. "Likes" and comments on Facebook replace personal conversations. Man has lost touch with himself, his emotional world, and others. The contact with nature and coaching with horses could restore this relationship.

The bully in a love relationship

FRANCESCA WANTED TO TRY the systemic horse-assisted coaching method but had no specific question. She told me that she sometimes worries about her son and wants a session about her life and what she could do to make her professional and private life more balanced. She also wanted to have a representative for her son.

The two horses kept walking between her "son" and her, spinning circles and even running again through the space in between the two. Walking between her and her son, the horses were very agitated, to a point where they pushed the "son" and her farther apart. There was a clear theme here about boundaries and respect for each other's space.

She told me that her place in her life was not respected. Francesca talked about her father, and I asked for a representative for her father. As soon as her "father" came in, the horses suddenly went wild. They ran in circles and even stepped on a wasp nest in the meadow, thus causing even more turbulence and causing people from outside to rush in to calm the horses and drive the wasps away. Francesca recognized her father in this behavior, always restless and in disharmony, just like her partner, who had left her and her son years ago.

In this session, an intervention was made between Francesca and her father, creating a balance between give-and-take and the unnecessary burden that belonged to her father. She noted that she had unconsciously chosen a partner that resembled her father, with his lack of stability and great dominance. By "giving back" what came from her father, she was able to take her life back into her own hands. As soon as she focused on this procedure and set limits, the horses calmed down.

Through this experience, I also realized my own turbulent relationships and was able to create new boundaries in my life.

The interesting thing about this situation is that horses will always show what is important for the development of the coachee at the given moment, even if the person has no question at all. Francesca hinted at the end of the session that she had indeed been very busy on the subject of boundaries, both in her private and professional life.

Horses just have this extraordinary power to live and sense the here and now.

Controlled first love

MARIO, THE OWNER OF the equitation sports center, had no question. When I asked him what aspect of his life he wanted to know more about, he said, "Let's just see what the horses will tell me." When he took his place in the field, he immediately preferred a very central, open place in the arena: "That way I can see my whole environment and control everything."

The two horses remained at a distance from him and avoided contact, which is an indication that the person does not really give himself to how he feels. The horses stood perfectly next to each other. They showed some order, eating grass and slowly moving away from him. When I asked him for an explanation, he said that he likes to focus on "reason" and "the mind" and that everything in his life and work is well organized. And what about his emotions or feelings in life?

Mario was silent for a moment and then said he was feeling uncomfortable. The horses moved closer to him, which is a sign that the person is getting more focused on how he or she feels. Mario had identified himself most with the white horse, which symbolized his mind. To the brown he felt less attracted, and just that horse now confronted him. That made him unsure.

I asked him why control was so important to him. He admitted he had to deal with fear and insecurity in his professional life, the risk every time when he had to jump with a horse, the feeling of competition, and come up to expectations of his audience and family. He always had to emit a good impression to the outside world.

The moment he admitted his feelings of insecurity, the brown horse went up to him and bent its neck very softly and vulnerably. It easily touched Mario's right leg, which stands for the masculinity—control and assertiveness.

I first appointed two representatives, two persons, for his "reason" and "heart", in order to obtain more information. "Reason" stood next to Mario; the "heart" hid behind reason. I asked him to first contact his heart; Mario still felt uncomfortable and unstable, but he felt better the moment he stood beside reason.

Another representative, a person for Mario's "fear," came in. When he took his hands off reason and heart, he could face fear. He recognized his fear and accepted it. The two horses stood around him, and the brown horse placed Mario in the foal position, a sign of protection in the moment he felt emotionally vulnerable. After this intervention, Mario felt more balance within and was free to embrace his heart.

A simple session; however, it revealed the man's life dilemma in earlier love relationships and in his work, which he later admitted. The session set his inner functioning in motion and connected reason more with his heart, his true life engine. Weeks later, he told me that he already felt more open to his inner voice and appreciated the emotional aspects of life a lot more.

Israel

ACTUALLY, I HAPPENED TO have landed in Israel by coincidence, but I spent a lot of time there, and learned Hebrew as well as Arabic. It was exciting to participate in intercultural peace projects, when I got to know the advanced, high-tech world there as well, and made new contacts. In my conversations and interactions, I felt that this country had lost a certain softness, which aroused very paradoxical feelings in me. The history of the country is fascinating, but politically and philosophically, it is very controversial. It is a country that has had no separation of state and religion since its inception, with a government and society that is gradually becoming more fanatical, nationalist, religious, and indoctrinated with militant bravura and patriarchal principles.

As such, the emotional world is thereby neglected. When we talk about empathy in politics, only a few Israeli journalists, like Gideon Levy and Uri Avnery, criticize the current situation in society very sharply and alert their readers to the danger.

Due to historical-systemic causes, this country depends on a role it cannot get out of and which can only be viewed from one side. This becomes clear in school lessons and in military training, where a certain ideal picture predominates that must not be questioned. One can imagine that this has an effect on everyday life. Added to this is a fear of terrorism and emphasis on defensive action—at least to be prepared for it.

The journalist Edith Lutz, in het book Grenzgänge im Januar (Border-crossings in January) for example, also sees the need to intensify the peace process with mediators and systemic consultants.

I also believe that only by confronting fear and prejudice and assuming responsibility for oneself can we remedy the situation, even on the collective, social level!

It is a given in psychology that the boundaries between being a victim and a perpetrator are very diffuse and grey: throughout history, it is notable that often, a traumatized victim turns into a perpetrator. The challenge of man is to go beyond that in the subjective as well as collective field and to heal these feelings in oneself. To rise above the fears and undergo a healing process is only possible through love and acceptance.

The feminine side of society, empathy and connection with others, including the Palestinians, seems to be controlled by anachronistic, patriarchal systems. Consequently, the philosophy of life is associated with dogmatic religion and nationalist ideas. In Israeli society, animals are often considered inferior, some even as impure, especially in the Arab and Orthodox Jewish worlds. Many Jewish or Arab people would not consider coaching with animals, because they believe they are above the animal and an animal thus cannot teach humans.

In the private sector, I met many warm people who did not shy away from physical contact and spontaneity. I experienced a loose Mediterranean way like the Italians have, but it stops where the national interest or religion comes into the conversation. Family life revolves around traditional ideas. Even the horses showed this aspect very clearly—an environment in which love, power of the heart, and true spiritual freedom have yet to find their way. Nevertheless, we have been able to find a few open-minded people who were amazed at the accurate and correct reactions of the horses and other animals! The animals will certainly carry on their work in the future to give again their place to the soft and tender side of this land!

A world between words

RONIT WANTED TO HAVE some coaching experience and was curious about her relationship with her husband. A horse stood by the water well and kept drinking. Ronit mentioned that she often talked to her husband about everything that needs to be said and tries to cover all aspects. Reading between words is nonsense, her husband had said. She had not agreed with him and felt that she was not being taken seriously. Interestingly, the words "emotions" or "feelings" were never mentioned by her during this session; it was more like a dialogue about semantics.

I asked her to watch the horse and tell me what she saw.

"Drinking water. He has to be thirsty," she said.

"And what about you?" I asked. I mentioned that this could also mean a need for life-energy, for emotions.

"Yes, maybe," she said. Her father would have been like her husband; he was not very accessible and did not speak at all about his feelings. The word "emotion" did not seem to resonate with her.

A representative for her father came in, and Ronit found it difficult to look into his eyes. The horse, which was drinking all the time, turned to her. A sudden reaction usually implies an inner authentic movement. "It's all right with my dad," she said, "and I'm fine too."

Somehow, I avoided the emotional confrontation with her father and the horse. I felt that I needed to take another path to her heart.

"I just want my daughter to be happy." Her daughter was the first in the family who did not care what people said and cared only about her freedom. When Ronit started talking about her, a playful dog came in next to her. "That could be my daughter," said Ronit. "She's as playful as a dog." She suddenly had tears in her eyes. The horse stood quietly beside her.

For Ronit, this intervention of her daughter was the most important thing. She wanted her daughter to follow her heart and not be constrained by her parents, with too many words or strict rules. She sincerely wished for her daughter a different life and a good partner relationship. The two horses remained standing next to her, and that moved her to tears in the moment as she wished her daughter all the love she herself had not received. Horses just want us to show our vulnerable, true side: masks are instantly recognized and removed in order to focus on the essence, the true nature of humans.

The absent father

THE SURPRISING THING ABOUT coaching with horses is that, often by coincidence, or rather, in the interconnection of sudden circumstances, the coachee, the representative, and the horses are all healed, and all participants heal each other. Or, as I always like to say, they make each other "whole" again.

For a long time, I had tried to invite a friend of mine to a coaching. She had often told me that it was important to her to experience such a systemic horse coaching. One day, we finally managed to make an appointment. She told me she was feeling depressed; nothing in her life was as she wished. Her work gave her some pleasure, but since her husband had left her and returned to Russia, she felt a great vacuum.

Coincidentally, an Israeli friend of mine was present to be a representative. He had suffered a severe divorce, losing both his possessions and his children through legal disputes at the rabbinical court, which still governs with outdated biblical laws in deciding whether a divorce should take place or not. The children had decided against him and done everything to make his life impossible. "My children are dead," he said often; this would be the dark side of the society of Israel, with no separation of religion and state. Lawyers use old religious laws and arguments to finish off an adversary.

The woman positioned herself in the arena and explained that she needed something in the back, a support, like in her life. The little horse stood briefly with her but disappeared again. All the others disappeared and hid back in the stable.

There was distance in her life; could she recognize that?

"Yes," she said. "Nobody was interested in me when I was little. I had to do everything as expected." We walked to the stable to check the horses. The little horse was blocked by the others and could not get out. She recognized herself in it. Her father had always ignored her and was just busy with his work.

I asked her where she was in the whole picture. She did not know, but she soon saw the little horse standing far away from her.

As a representative for her father, she brought out the friend. He was not involved at all and did not know what he was doing there. He also considered everything emotional or psychological as a kind of nonsense.

"That's what my father would say now."

She could finally look the "father" in the eye, accept him as he was, and give the "negative burden" back to him. His problems were his, and she would not have to carry them any longer.

She looked at the little horse again, and I asked her to pick a representative for her heart. The woman who stood for her heart immediately started to cry and positioned herself far away from her.

"That's it," the coachee recognized emotionally. "I abandoned my own heart, my own emotional needs!" She walked toward her "heart" and made contact. At that moment, the horse stood between the two and made a move from one's hand to the other as a sign to really connect.

The woman who represented the heart told me she felt relieved. She would have always been afraid of losing control in life, and that would have happened to her now. She had lost control and even burst into tears. But she did not feel bad at all now, but much better.

The man who symbolized her father responded evasively to my question. But the confrontation with a "daughter" had already touched him. It was also striking that the "daughter" remembered her father much as the man had portrayed him: distanced, workaholic, distracted.

Humans are the way they are, and here the horses work without judgment. It is just the way it is, and that's good. This acceptance, this unconditional love gives humans, the coachees, the freedom to develop further.

The aftermath of the coaching lasts a long time after the sessions, as we know from practice. The participants apparently change something unconsciously in their emotional world, in their behavior pattern, and in their system, and the effect is therefore sustainable. We cannot really explain it yet, but many people report some kind of relief, new ideas, memories, and inspirations that change their lives, a wonderful sign that the mind is linked to the unconscious emotional world.

How connected are we?

EXPERIENCES WITH SYSTEMIC HORSE-ASSISTED coaching in different countries and cultures show certain tendencies in each country that reflect the typical behaviors of a culture but also the extraordinary universal language of horses and nature in general, which gives place everywhere to every person or creation, without any judgment, through the power of the heart.

According to the systemic laws, there are three basic principles:

1) Every person is part of a system—his or her family, the environment, and his or her professional background

2) Every person has a specific role and function and his or her own place. For example, each system has its own order with its own specific rules, such as in the family, the older person goes before the younger person, or the one who has been in a company for the longest time has priority over the other employees.

3) In these systems, whether family or business, we must talk about a balance between give and take. When one gives more

than the other, there is a lack of balance and one cannot properly take one's place in life to live one's authentic power.

Being able to receive, is as important as being able to give.

Are you able to receive a well meant compliment? Are you able to take a loss, for example the inability of a parent to give you enough attention, a fact you cannot change in life?

The same goes for giving, if, for example, you unconsciously give yourself away too much and take on another person's burden, living the life of the other person. You take the burden into your own life and do not realize that you are being blocked by it in your further decisions and activities. This is not really your burden, but it is becoming more and more to be regarded as your own. This can become a real blind spot to many people, especially in relationships, where one projects misinterpretations or beliefs and pains onto the partner.

This phenomenon can last for generations, with many unconsciously passing on a pain without ever analyzing it and without "giving it back" to the other person in the system. Personal pain is something for which every human being should take responsibility by looking into the pain, feeling it, and giving it its place. This place is often with the parents, siblings, or grandparents.

Children absorb the signals of their environment like a sponge. These signals are unconsciously processed. These are signals that lead to certain patterns and usually do not serve the happiness of people, and then these patterns repeatedly appear and thus disturb either one's professional life or a personal relationship. These patterns prevent the individual from living his or her full personal potential and taking his or her place as a full-fledged, authentic person with light and dark sides.

It is always interesting to see how connected we are to each other, how every person who is not in balance influences others. Just a group of people—for example, a family—lives without being aware of their blind spots. Replacing misinterpretations with positive ideas and feelings can further influence an even larger environment.

The same is true of horses: as said before, if not every horse takes its own place and has access to its authentic abilities, the rest of the herd must compensate for it; ultimately the common interest prevails. Therefore, breaking through old patterns, unconscious blockages, thoughts, and feelings is so essential for society.

This is another reason to pay special attention to the inner emotional balance of people in education, the school system, and society. The development of empathic, emotional skills is demonstrably extremely important, even for schools, in politics, and in the sustainable enterprise; it would even help to reduce costs in health and social care!

For that reason, I would suggest to have more focus on private relations instead of public relations! Have effective, profound communication instead of slogans and short elevator pitches! Social skills balance between assertiveness and empathy.

Exercise role-playing—"walk in the shoes of the other"—and thus put yourself in the place of the other in different situations. Use active listening instead of a competitor's mentality! We need personality development, in which reason and intuition are combined with feeling and every child, every citizen, is convinced that their authentic abilities have added value and are in demand in society.

What exactly is the feeling of "inner wisdom"?

⁘

REGULARLY, THE TERM FEELING, or intuition, has been used here. It could raise a question to people, namely, are all feelings really good and constructive? Including feelings of hatred, anger, and bitterness?

Let's start by saying that feelings are, first and foremost, subjective. They belong to life, to humans, and determine their reactions, which of course can be very primeval and even aggressive as a result.

But as horses show in many coaching sessions, reactions and feelings are always a consequence of certain events or developments in childhood, a product of different situations and people in life, and often, behind a feeling of anger and bitterness is a whole world of pain, like the pain of being abandoned by others. Proven or not, feelings should not simply be pushed to the side but analyzed and the motives behind them revealed.

The dualistic thing about us human beings is that we call situations in life and also feelings either bad or good, and therefore, many authentic situations or feelings are not really experienced—or valued as such. One dares not to look them in the eye. The right path of development often leads inward, into our own consciousness, deep into the dark chambers of our fear, distress, and sorrow as well!

Feelings like bitterness and hatred are mostly a consequence of other sensations. They are the impression of not being accepted, not being loved. The art is to accept a feeling in a situation, to embrace it in order to be able to let it go with unconditional love and without any judgment.

Instead, we push away certain feelings, consider them as "non-sense," or rationalize or describe them, out of pride or bitterness, which can also be described as "frozen" love, when the door to expressing emotions is completely locked, out of pain or experienced from the past. In any case, feelings are not recognized or labeled. Added to this is the fact that man has difficulty with embracing reason and feeling to really live in the present. We think, "Once I get my diploma, everything will be better ..." or, "Once I have a relationship, I will be really happy," and so on.

During a meeting with friends, you are not really present; instead, you think about what you have to do in the next few days: doing the laundry, painting the living room walls, preparing the tax return, etc. Do you recognize these thoughts and feelings, as well as the frustration caused by this constant pondering?

Eckhart Tolle, a spiritual teacher and author, writes in his work "The Power of Now" that body sensation, much more than the ego, the right "being" in the body, and the ability to understand the moment lead us to more hidden potential and could even heal the whole body.

A horse, on the other hand, lives completely in the present and always reacts exactly at the very moment when the coachee makes an inner movement and recognizes his or her situation in the present and the emotions connected with it. The horse then looks them in the eye and recognizes that the coachee feels sad, abandoned, or hopeless. In this magical moment, when a human being in vulnerability also holds onto this authentic power with both hands, the horse approaches the person and makes visible contact.

A fragmented world in search of "complement"

THE DIFFERENT SESSIONS IN different countries were about bringing people back into balance by eliminating barriers and unconscious inhibitions brought on by the system, often through the family system, where something had to be cured, healed, or supplemented.

These mental wounds are usually the reason that relationships are not going well, because humans intuitively somehow and usually unconsciously want to cover up or compensate for wounds, memories, and pain. This healing and the opening up of new potential and options are only possible if not only the mind is involved but especially the unconscious emotional world and the intuition in which misinterpretations were unconsciously stored and hidden. Without the sometimes difficult and painful journey into your own inner self and down into your own world of shadows in order to consciously feel and accept old pain, complete healing is not possible.

Pierre, a civil engineer, had always traveled a lot. "Choose a good horse for me," he said, without realizing that coaching is not dependent on good riding horses.

He stood in the middle of the ring and looked at Tanka, the horse who immediately turned away from him. Tanka ran to the edge of the ring and stopped there, as if he wanted to go out, then directed his gaze into the distance.

Did Pierre himself go out somewhere? Was he in the right place in his life?

He admitted that he did not feel good where he lived now. He would rather be in the countryside. Unfortunately, his partner had little understanding for this. Pierre suddenly seemed to be another man. He told about the quarrels with his partner. The horse Tanka came closer and closer. In the end, Tanka nibbled on Pierre's sweater, something that mostly refers to the fact that it would take care of Pierre.

"Yes," he said. "That's an issue in the relationship." He would not care enough about her, which was the accusation of his wife, or about taking care of himself.

I had the man set up a representative for his partner. Intuitively, the woman stood far away from the husband.

I asked Pierre to look at his partner, but he could not concentrate on her. He had to admit, he felt alien to her.

Somehow, he had trouble getting in touch with himself; apparently he just wanted to get away—even away from himself?

He identified himself with Tanka, so I asked him again to touch the horse and feel his skin, his warmth. This allowed him to come back to himself. He had tears in his eyes. Every word could have been too much.

I just turned him gently toward his partner so he could look at her and feel his feelings for her. He stayed at a distance.

"She's still far away," he said, but it would be OK like that.

You can only really open someone's heart when the person is ready for it, and that takes time. But the emotional first step had been made.

Also, in my experience, many psychotherapeutic and coaching projects were often only partially successful, because you did not pay enough attention to the essence of what was said. One tests, talks, or tries "mindfulness," but as the name implies, you remain at the level of the rational mind, and thus you cannot fully analyze deeper feelings, especially the unconscious dark ones, in order to empathize and live through and correct such at the body sensation level, or "felt sense," as it is so expressively said in English.

We can also see the same pattern happening in society. Feelings at the collective level should be recognized, discussed, and balanced. These feelings, the unconscious behavior of the collective, are a result of all people, with their (family) systems and their history. As soon as there is great frustration here, which is a reflection of the inner part of society as a whole, there will be a policy that will refuse to face this frustration in order to address it properly. The fear of the majority of people is used by politicians, to split society, thereby putting more power in the hands of these politicians. Fear is translated into aggression. Here, too, it is important not to push the feelings aside but to look at the light and dark sides and deal with them constructively.

We see these phenomena especially in nowadays politics. which are expressed in populism, currents that frantically cling to national values or exclusive groups that could turn into an aggressive force on their own, just like a person whose pride or self-esteem is totally hurt and who can then transform into a hard and even aggressive, unempathetic person. It's fascinating how this parallel is established in politics and society generally. There is no victim role without an attacker, and these roles alternate in history. Especially when hurt feelings at the collective level are ignored, these become larger and will be gradually less controllable over time.

A kind of routine thinking and acting silently permeates without being noticed! Politicians are clearly losing touch with the needs of the population and are only spouting their own programs. They only talk to each other at meetings, and one often wonders if any one of them is interested in only his or her own agenda or truly in the ideals that should make the lives of those who elected him or her better.

If an existing policy has not taken the frustrations of society seriously and established no dialogue with society, as could be possible with committees where the citizens are involved, this fact will only be ammunition for the populist parties, which will only gain more votes.

That is why I am convinced that this kind of mediation can be used as an effective link between people and politics nowadays and is an absolute necessity. Specifically in mediation, we slow down the process by taking a step back and taking the feelings and frustrations seriously, starting with the motives and finally reaching a consensus for all whose bases could be useful to the politicians, as well as the electorate.

And then we come to the sensitive point of religion, a topic that still plays an important role in today's society: which religion is the right one? Almost as if to say, who are the "chosen people" now, or who has a monopoly on truth? Is this not suggesting a definitive discrimination? During my time in Israel, I was able to study monotheistic religions more closely, both their differences and universal wisdom.

From my gut feeling, I was searching for the wisdom that unites all peoples and historical narratives, an element that resonates with

most of us, if not everyone, and conveys a positive sense of acceptance and connection. All religious teachings basically have many
interfaces and have brought forth thinkers and leaders to apply a
general or universal wisdom for humanity, even though religions
themselves always claim exclusivity for their own group.

In Judaism, in the Proverbs of the Fathers in the Talmud, a concentrate of Jewish wisdom, we read the following:

וְאַל תָּדִין אֶת חֲבֵרְךָ עַד שֶׁתַּגִּיעַ לִמְקוֹמוֹ

"And do not judge your fellow until you have stood in his place"
(Pirkei Avot 2:5).

עַל שְׁלֹשָׁה דְבָרִים הָעוֹלָם עוֹמֵד, עַל הַדִּין וְעַל הָאֱמֶת וְעַל הַשָּׁלוֹם, שֶׁנֶּאֱמַר
(זכריה ח) אֱמֶת וּמִשְׁפַּט שָׁלוֹם שִׁפְטוּ בְּשַׁעֲרֵיכֶם:

"On three things does the world stand: On justice, truth, and
peace, as it is said: "execute the judgment of truth and peace in
your gates" (Pirkei Avot 1:18).

In the Qur'an, we find,

يَا أَيُّهَا النَّاسُ إِنَّا خَلَقْنَاكُم مِّن ذَكَرٍ وَأُنثَى وَجَعَلْنَاكُمْ شُعُوباً وَقَبَائِلَ لِتَعَارَفُوا إِنَّ أَكْرَمَكُمْ
عِندَ اللهِ أَتْقَاكُمْ إِنَّ اللهَ عَلِيمٌ خَبِيرٌ

"O humankind! Surely We have created you from a single
(pair of) male and female, and made you into tribes and families
so that you may know one another (and so build mutuality and
co-operative relationships, not so that you may take pride in your
differences of race or social rank, or breed enmities). Surely the

noblest, most honorable of you in God's sight is the one best in piety, righteousness, and reverence for God. Surely God is All-Knowing, All-Aware." (49:13).

The differences between people exist so that people can get to know each other and support each other, not so that they deny each other or are in conflict with each other. Among other things, a milestone is set in the Qur'an concerning social life. Differences between different peoples are natural and they should not serve as an obstacle but as a way to approach each other. The explicit commandment of godliness in this context also underlines the importance of mutual tolerance.

The Bible mentions both charity and self-love: you must love your neighbor as yourself (Leviticus 19:1718).

As the Bible reveals, it is appropriate and even necessary to love oneself to a reasonable degree. This love includes self-esteem, caring for oneself, and an awareness of one's own worth (Matthew 10:31). Instead of glorifying egoism, the Bible places self-love in the right place. If you do not love yourself, you cannot love others in a healthy way.

Are not these all very current sayings in this day and age?

PEOPLE HAVE BEEN KILLING each other for centuries in the name of their respective religion. Obviously, every religion began as a kind of exclusive club, in which other groups were excluded because of patriarchal dogmas. The power of certain elites and the religious dogmas were accepted by a crowd again and again, out of either fear or ignorance. Unfortunately, this is a thinking that still exists.

People often felt they were not masters of their own mind, feeling, or life. One did not need to think for oneself or shape one's life and relationships; the God Almighty or the religious institutions were there to arrange everything.

It is my believe that today we should be dealing with a more universal spirituality or life philosophy, a spirituality that connects based on love and acceptance, in which mankind is seen as the responsible creator of society and his life, and in this context, the power of love is considered a "divine spark." "Trust in God" could as well be a trust in the good of human beings and should come from the inside, not from the outside. The answers to many questions and problems lie within our own being, not outside. Even in nature, development is from the inside out, as with the bird crawling out of the egg and the child coming forth from the mother's womb.

It is precisely through one's own emotional world, physical sensation, and the power of love that we, each in our own way, can better discover our spirituality through art, music, nature, and the healing power of horses, thereby also achieving greater compatibility in our international society!

Mediation: Solve conflicts with empathy and logic

WE ALL KNOW THEM: conflicts at work, in the family, or between neighbors, who can end up in court to the bitter end. Lawyers represent the interests of one party, and they look for omissions and anomalies in procedure to bring the opponent's party to its knees.

In the end, perhaps one legal battle has been won and a good sum of money was secured, but basically both parties often end up as losers. Such court procedures not only cost a lot of money, time, and negative energy, but the relationship and human contact with the other party can be lost forever.

Creating division is the goal of this process in order for a party to win, and all clauses and laws are used and sometimes even abused for the sake of a one-sided profit.

But you should understand this correctly; in some cases, a lawyer or the legal system is certainly important in resolving issues, but in many cases, it is a shortcoming in communication or in human connection. Lawyers focus only on the dividing aspects instead of looking at the motives of the two parties and encouraging them to listen to each other first in order to come to a workable solution.

In these cases, mediation can be a good solution, because it is not a legal process but a communication process that slows down the development of tension and blockages at the onset of the conflict and discusses the feelings and motives of the two parties in order to build mutual understanding where communication and creativity can flow again. Common motives can then be maintained again, and both can continue to coexist.

With this method, however, a completely different mindset is required of the mediator than that of a lawyer. An attorney who wants to end up settling, compromising between the two, ultimately focuses on the profits of his or her party and does not aim for mutual gain. You focus again on the wrong steps and deficiencies of the other.

Some lawyers, though, have learned a good mediation technique. Nevertheless, it is almost impossible in the legal, rather divisive process to suddenly cultivate a connecting mindset. This makes the lawyer's motives and purpose suddenly questionable at a certain stage of the process.

A mediator should be neutral from the beginning and should have the connecting factor of synergy as the ideal goal.

This can be a big challenge, because after all, there are also personal blind spots, so-called systemic patterns, which somehow must be worked out by the person him- or herself, or with another in systemic coaching, because the same problems come along very differently, and conflicts will repeat themselves.

In general, a mediation process leads to many good results, where, thanks to the special technique, parties can speak out, misunderstandings can be clarified, and relationships can be improved.

Add to this the fact that a mediation contract also has legal binding force—but even with the consent of both parties—and thus results in much more than a constructive basis for the resolution of the conflict and an improved relation between the two parties!

As an interpreter, my experience in the legal process was often quite stressful. Of course, I loved switching from one language and culture to another, but for me it was more of an exciting challenge to be a connecting factor, and having felt the miscommunication between the parties involved was frustrating.

The legal process, however, always filled me with negative emotions, as if the connecting human element were becoming more and more nonexistent. It was not generally communicated with empathy and compassion but primarily with hard facts, quotes, and verdicts.

The lawyer would try to stage his show as well as possible, attempting to destroy the other party or their interests. Once, the judge even shouted at a party! This certainly also indicated that the court system is overstrained and judges have to work under the influence of burnout symptoms, something that does not promote balance and justice as a whole.

More and more, I got the feeling that these court sessions are not really up to date anymore. We have reached a time when people should take up responsibility for creating a society with an interest in dialogue, a true democracy with sustainable solutions, with educational opportunities for those who are at the top of personality development to create the opportunity for people to develop their own ethical feelings and empathy for themselves and others. When building a society, we must never forget that we are all connected; the well-being of one person is directly dependent on other people and groups—especially in this global world!

Mediation or public diplomacy in society and politics

"THERE'S BEEN ANOTHER CLASS cancellation at school, and one of us has to stay home, at least to check Chris's homework," Stephen said, irritated, to his wife. He put his arm around her. Since the systemic coaching session, they had learned to communicate better, always in conjunction with each other. They had learned that although some moments may be annoying, it should always be possible to listen to one another with attention and love.

"Oh, this is the physics teacher Chris always talks about," smiled Cybil, "who often has a nervous breakdown. Frankly, it is also very stressful in the classroom. Many are simply overworked. His physics lesson has been cancelled before. I think the organization at school is pretty chaotic anyway. There never seems to be money for the right things. Chris always mentions that their lessons are boring and without any practice."

In politics, there is little talk of improvement or more budget for education. When you need new colleagues in a team, you are often disappointed with the lack of up-to-date knowledge or creativity in the students, and language skills are often pretty lacking.

Is this just regarded as merely a profit-and-loss business?

Is there a lack of vision, or does it have to do with neoliberal ideas, where you think spending needs to go down?

Training is seen in society as a cost model rather than an added-value model, where you want to bring in as much as possible without much effort. Of course, this is not the case. Parents cannot be expected to organize their own private schools. Schools should respond to a minimum of requirements and offer quality education to all.

It has been forgotten that investing in public expenditures, such as good quality schooling and promoting culture, repays itself through well-educated people, a positive impact on society, and fewer social issues.

Culture and science form a society and promote creativity and new ideas. Unfortunately, this is currently less the case in several European countries. Workers in the arts and cultural scene are often worried about their jobs, since art is being increasingly regarded as an obsolete luxury, though this sector has so much importance to society and its identity and in developing empathic skills and creativity.

Max was particularly concerned with the question of how he could again be active as an orchestra conductor in music. Times are quite difficult in the art industry.

He talked about his career and the many challenges that eventually drove him out of his job and forced him to go elsewhere. There were many words and explanations. So I asked him to regain his calmness in this session and then continue.

It became clear to me how important it was for him to experience the whole process, with the associated feelings and focusing much more on his felt sense and less on his brain.

Juan, the lively Lusitano horse, remained uninterested all the time, on the edge of the ring, nibbling grass. Olaf, the strong Frisian horse, first stood next to Max but slowly walked away during the conversation, nibbling grass without interruption, a sign of wanting food, as well as mental food and making himself useful. I asked Max if he recognized this situation. Did the inclusion of mental food make sense to him? He admitted that he wanted to keep evolving and working out new projects for management, but he clearly missed the music, with which he cannot make enough money right then.

Olaf continued to graze while Max talked about this shortage of money and how he lost his luck in the music industry and so urgently needed to find other work.

He wished now for new opportunities, contacts, and start-up capital to find a new ensemble. Olaf did not change his attitude; he continued to eat continuously, as if under stress, and signaled no opening or new possibilities. The dialogue remained at the intellectual level.

It was clear that this conversation did not lead to a solution and to the main theme or new insights. Next, I asked Max what his biggest blockage was. He replied, "The fear that things will not turn out well." At that moment, he seemed to be feeling more. He seemed looser and less tense in his posture. There were more moments of silence.

I then asked him to set up an object for his fear, give it a place, and focus on it. He felt the energy of that fear and became a little more nervous.

As a balance, I asked him to put something in that had a positive influence on him. He then pointed to his heart, symbolizing his inspiration, and assigned it to a traffic cone. He actually felt better the moment he grabbed the traffic cone.

At the same time, the horse turned. Olaf walked in the direction of Max and made contact with his hands. Usually this is a sign of the horse pushing the coachee to come into action and make a new move. Did Max work enough with his inspiration? He did not know.

Then Olaf turned around and turned his back on Max. He dangled his genital organ and stood in front of the "fear" constrictor.

The rump usually represents the lower chakras of a human or animal and, in combination with the growing sexual organ, especially the sacral chakra. The sacral chakra is in connection with sexuality, creativity, and the feeling of contact with humans.

According to old Hindu teachings, but also in other ancient cultures, a chakra is one of the seven energy centers of spiritual power in the human body. These streams of energy penetrate the physical body and connect it with the spirit of man, the astral body.

I asked Max if these were relevant topics in his life, issues that might have worried him.

His reaction was a bit embarrassed. The deeper contact with others would be an issue. "Maybe," he said, but somehow he could not comment on it. The silence was very beneficial for me and also for Max, as he seemed to relax more.

Quite spontaneously, the question came up of his parents and his relationship with them. Max had fully broken off any contact because of arguments with his mother some years ago. Unfortunately, such a break with the parents or confidants in the life of a person often has serious consequences and can have much influence on later contacts.

As soon as he mentioned his mother and a representative came into the ring as his mother, suddenly the horse Juan, who had been standing on the outside for a long time, without moving, turned and stood next to Max and the mother.

Juan pushed Max's head down a bit, as if he were allowed to be small again, and then leaned against his body, as if he wanted to give Max his heart-energy. Moved, Max stood there with so much love and such a meaningful message.

Although he found it difficult, he looked at his mother, who told him she was suffering from the breakup. She told him that she loved him but also had her own problems that were in her way and that she could not express herself well. Tears rolled down the cheeks of both Max and the mother.

I asked Max if he could see his mother and accept her as she is and give her back the unnecessary burden. This was the burden that should not be his burden, her own frustrations and inhibitions. He did this symbolically with a stone and felt the burden before he returned it to her. "I want to live my life in freedom," he said.

In this intervention, something was done that had not yet happened or may perhaps never happen in reality, but it changed the energy and intentions, and unconscious feelings in the coachee. These words were important because they carried an intention that could be integrated through it. In many cases, you actually notice a change in the patterns and beliefs of a coachee, and therefore in their other contacts and in their openness to establishing contact.

Without the initial anxiety, the lack of self-confidence that comes, for the most part, from the mother relationship, Max would find it much easier to deal with new challenges in music.

He mentioned months later that his contacts somehow flowed more fluently. He found new opportunities, especially in the music field, where you have to deal with many emotional people, and he could now find his place in it better, and new projects came to him! Yes, it is precisely this changing to a deeper and greater consciousness that will bring much to humanity in the future.

We live in a time of change and big development, where old systems can somehow no longer be upheld. Old structures and thinking systems are increasingly questioned.

But it is also a time when money and power, as well as old patriarchal values, are still the controlling forces in society and politics. Looking at developments in the world, both national and regional, one has the feeling that the individual citizen has lost control of the system. People are often no longer informed, or they feel a kind of frustration during or after elections, because either way (one thinks), the big organizations and coalitions of politicians make the decisions. Some citizens may not even take part in the elections, or they may organize themselves into a few "grassroots" movements but have nothing to say formally.

How much influence does the citizen really have? Where is the idealism of politicians? Have we all forgotten that the state and politicians should be at the service of the citizens? Where have the "matriarchal," empathic values in society gone? It is clear that a great distance was created between society and politicians. What could be changed in this situation? Here, mediation or conflict mediation would be the solution of the future!

Many politicians can be seen trying to get things right and pushing through their point of view. This is a tough, nonempathic process that we recognize very well in the courtroom. It leads to a situation in which even the winner of the procedure does not feel good about it. It neglects many elements: sociological, communication, scientific, and psychological backgrounds!

It is also interesting to see how policymakers consider it their task to persuade citizens to adopt their point of view. Unfortunately, this is the opposite of what democracy should be! Democracy is about developing solutions together by looking at people's needs and the broad, general common good.

The main question in a conflict is this: what brings me to this position? Which need is really behind it? Afterward, many people notice that—despite different points of view—there is common ground on the "need" level. The task of politicians in democracy would be to carry these needs into policy and constructively build solutions on this basis.

With mediation in civil society and awareness-raising of empathy within society, one could return to the very essence of democracy. On the one hand, mediation is a process; on the other hand, it is a toolbox with various communication and negotiation instruments.

In the past, citizen participation was something that was introduced and discussed. After that, it fell to what a few people thought was right. As a result, there is more and more resignation in the people and a significant lack of confidence.

Mediation or civil engineering tools could improve the situation for the citizen. It would provide a framework in which all the important points of society and political issues are put on the table and appreciation is maintained. Of course, this topic should be discussed already in school and in all education. The citizen should be emancipated, well-informed, and aware of his responsibility of the ramifications of his ballot-choice!

It would be an excellent thing if assemblies and committees were public—not public sessions but public citizen committee meetings. At first, perhaps only a few citizens would be present, but if people feel that it is an honest opportunity to get involved, to shape the government, and to be taken seriously, a boardroom would fill up very quickly, and trust would be restored!

Another main question would be, again and again, "What is important to the citizen?" And the politician would listen for the first time and later be authorized to continue to accompany the whole process. The consciousness of the people would grow, and the challenges in society could be dealt with, and resolved.. Mediation would undoubtedly open new avenues for more justice in society in this process!

Lack of empathy development in education: "An avalanche is approaching us"

IN WONDERFUL WEATHER, OF course I like to ride on my horse Olaf through nature in the Clape. All of a sudden, a cyclist drives past my horse very close and at high speed. It is startled, scared, and jumps uncontrollably aside for a moment, but the cyclist continues without any shown interest.

These scenes are common, both in adults and children. Children intentionally throwing balls and not paying attention to how an animal will react, along with other phenomena that merely show a lack of empathy (e.g., bullying in class), is a situation where children demonstrate their frustrations. If they are not encouraged to think about others' feelings, to empathize with others, then later, in professional life, they continue this behavior.

There are always conflicts between children. But how many have learned how to solve a conflict or misunderstanding and improve their relationships?

Another important question: how many personality-forming subjects are there in schools? These would be subjects in which you slowly, and not only at the intellectual level but also at the level of emotions, discover who you are, get to know your talents and weaknesses, and recognize them not as an absolute given but as properties that can always change. Also, you would learn to embrace both the positive and the dark sides. This gives every single child the right impulses and strengthens their self-confidence.

It is also interesting that in America, when asked where the milk comes from—and you will be amazed—most children indeed think that milk is simply coming from the supermarket. Especially in these societal systems, such as the school system, we have lost our relationship with nature, forgetting the relation to our own feelings and, at the same time, our relation to other human beings.

And there is something more fascinating; ask yourself the question, "How much knowledge have you kept from your school days, exactly?" You will see that these things were usually in the subjects for which you felt enthusiasm or motivation through curiosity or interest. Learning only has value if it is recorded with passion and enthusiasm.

This passion is usually not there, as you can see from how many students are not motivated. Some of the students therefore drop out of school prematurely and will never get a high school diploma.

There is also another point: how many programs really exist in school to develop children's emotional intelligence? Where are empathy and compassion actually formed? Education is only one half, in which the brain is fed with theses and theories. But the body sensation, the sensitivity—just the empathy—is not taught in our education systems at all. We cannot leave this challenge to politics alone. That is something we are all responsible for. The so-called responsible elite should be in touch with citizens and implement these new demands and ideas for education.

Per his study on empathy development in children, Dr. Karl Heinz Brisch, senior physician at the Pediatric and Polyclinic of the Ludwig-Maximilian University in Munich, Germany, said in an interview that we are finding more and more that children can no longer sufficiently empathize with others. It is expected to worsen in the coming years: there's an avalanche ahead of us.

Reasons for such a lack of empathizing skills among children are large nursery and daycare groups, increased demands, more administrative bureaucratic tasks for the educators, and many children with language problems. Many children are cared for a few weeks after birth in crèches with too few caretakers.

Empathy, according to Brisch is something very humanly necessary, otherwise we cannot have lasting, satisfying relationships, either with friends and partners, and later with children.

Usually, children learn empathy from parents and within well-functioning relationships. Otherwise, they would face great difficulties at school and with their classmates, and everywhere else. Studies in Austria with 250 elementary school children and in children's groups in Munich had led to the same results, finds Brisch.

Brisch also shows how priceless it is to bring children into contact with nature, animals, or vulnerable people such as infants. They really get in touch with their feelings and learn to empathize with others, to communicate, and also how much one can achieve with love and patience. A manager who is connected to his feelings acts more authentic and with integrity and has better contact with his team. A company with satisfied employees, where communication and atmosphere are valued, generally achieves better results.

Empathy is a trait that is, of course, only possible if a person also has empathy for him- or herself and if he or she does not have to constantly fight for his or her self-worth.

A leader who unconsciously doubts him- or herself can never use his or her full potential and is always worried about his or her existence and position. If a person constantly unconsciously thinks about the impression he or she makes and whether he or she has enough authority, this determines his or her behavior. He or she will constantly be afraid to fail and compensate for the uncertainty with an inauthentic or authoritarian attitude or mere facade. Who does not know the typically capricious or tyrannical boss who acts passive-aggressively, where the employee never really knows what's going on in the background? At the same time, the boss does not realize how the employees are doing.

But the power lies precisely in the vulnerability that allows one to communicate in an open, honest way, in which one can sometimes admit weaknesses or mistakes.

A manager with self-esteem who is aware of his strengths and weaknesses does not need to apply a mask in front of his employees!

A team also works better if the boss communicates positively, knows his or her own limits, and shows empathy, and it cannot be led by frustrations or projections.

In addition, a person with healthy self-esteem and communication skills is less at risk of burnout and automatically has more confidence in the people around him or her. It is through recognition and trust that the best in every person, in every team, is brought to the surface!

How horses react to self-love

JOHN, A BOY OF fourteen, was taken by his mother for systemic coaching with horses. His mother lamented his difficulty concentrating at school and his lack of self-confidence. He had been to a child psychologist, who talked to him a lot about his interests and his fears, but the boy did not seem to feel any better after the therapy. As an experiment, and also because the natural environment would give him peace, equine-assisted coaching was suggested to him.

A horse stood alone in the arena, and the boy was allowed to take his place there. He had previously said that he was a bit afraid of the horse. He was able to stroke and brush the horse with the coach in the stable. When he saw that the horse was quite calm and just sniffed something and licked his hand, he relaxed and smiled at the contact with the soft skin and the delicate nose of the horse.

In the ring, the horse stayed a little farther away from him. I asked him what he felt, if he would recognize it.

"The horse is alone there," he said.

"And you?" I asked.

"I'm often alone too," he said. "I do not have many friends; they stay away from me like the horse." John identified the horse emotionally and spontaneously with a potential friend.

In such a situation, the experience is that the horse then also emulates the energy of the so-called friend. I let John experience this feeling of loneliness again and encouraged him to really look at "not being good enough." John looked hurt and sad.

Then I asked him what he liked to do or when he would feel the best. "When I do my sudoku puzzles and assemble my model ships," he replied.

I asked him to close his eyes and fully imagine and remember that feeling of how proud and happy he was doing that, visualizing that pleasure in his own abilities as a warm light within himself.

John did so, and after a few seconds, the horse walked right up to him and stood in front of him, with his nose on his belly. John opened his eyes, and his look almost radiated. He had really experienced what it was like to feel self-love and what effect this had on the horse, his friend, or his environment!

It was a simple exercise that he could do in everyday life. A healthy self-confidence attracts people, especially those who share the same interests. It can be a first step to a more fulfilling life.

This is an example of how well animals can be used in therapeutic coaching or educational programs and how they help children in their development to become more balanced and therefore also responsible citizens who think about the general well-being of all people and choose politicians who they think are more sustainable and are truly engaged with society!

A little exercise for you, this time without horses

MAKE YOURSELF COMFORTABLE. TAKE a deep breath and imagine a ray of light directly above your head that penetrates the upper surface of your head, filling your whole body with white light and energy. Try to perceive this light of universal consciousness deep inside, its warmth and color. This light will strengthen you. Do the same with blue-colored light that represents your self-belief.

When you are completely relaxed, visualize the situations that give you a sense of happiness. Feel the atmosphere, the people, the environment, the smell, and the sounds and take in every detail. Try to keep the feeling as long as possible.

Sometimes ideas even come up that will help you.

This exercise can help with pressure and insecurity in an upcoming situation. You will see that after a few minutes you will feel calmer and more self-assured.

The big field: Horses show us tendencies and energy in today's society

IN THIS CHAPTER, I would like to focus on the macro-level connection, the connection in society, and the important role of nature and horses.

When working out a social question, we stood with a few colleagues in a field. A female systemic horse-assisted coach had invited her colleague—a shaman—to participate. As we have seen, in coaching or systemic work with horses, one can raise a certain question, but there is only one person who asks the question. In the course of the coaching process, horses may particularly show the elements or situations that are most important at that moment, the so-called "question behind the question." In my experience, horses only show what is most important for the person concerned, and it often touches the systemic causes.

For example, if a person wants to work on the question, "How do I earn more money in my job?" it may be—and this is usually the case—that the horses will first show this person where their potential blockages lie. These could be limiting thoughts or behavior that the coachee unconsciously inherited from his or her parents. This will, of course, be worked on first.

If you have worked through a certain systemic fact, you can continue. However, the horses will never stop working, and when a point is reached where the coachee has lived through his or her main theme in the present (also emotionally), one should then allow him or her the necessary time for internally processing all of it.

In the aforementioned case, the question was much more far-reaching. It was about the present situation in society—which forces are set in motion and which ones are neglected. I know that the word *shamanism* carries a connotation of occult practices, of magic and the intangible. However, shamanism is as old as humanity and, in particular, primarily closely connected to nature. Also, in shamanism, the shaman assumes a logical connection between humans and animals. Here, personal or social questions can be worked out and represented symbolically in a field, where everyone can assume a specific role spontaneously and intuitively; one follows his or her gut feeling or felt body sensation. There is more "wisdom" in the belly than one would expect. Nowadays, this method is being used more and more on corporate issues, and successfully, because it reveals invisible forces and the dynamics of an organization and offers new possibilities. Scientific studies confirm that everything is energy and vibration. Our energy is measurable and unlockable. For some time, biologists have recognized an energetic pattern in humans, animals, plants, and even dead material such as stones. But there is also mental energy that perhaps cannot yet be made directly visible through a laboratory test. Instead, the result, the vibration that emerges from the interaction with other people, is well recognizable.

As soon as we all had a place in the field, the horses came running toward us. The timing was perfect; at that moment we all consciously inhaled and exhaled and could follow our body feeling or intuition.

The horses showed a turbulent situation and came in with a kind of fighting spirit. Only the mare, who clearly stood for the "soft skills" element in society (empathy, connection, and love) stood on the hill beside the ring and seemed to oversee and dominate the whole scene. Then she joined the other horses, who were walking around or standing in the ring. The participants would also simply follow their physical feelings and go to a spot they felt drawn to.

The mares were scattered in the middle, and the geldings as well; it resulted in a confused situation where participants were sometimes driven in an easterly direction—the east wind direction being associated with action—but were again, during discussions, moved to the north—i.e., the direction of thought, or reason—and in the west section of the arena.

A woman in the northwest area felt weak and had to sit down to balance the constant flow of thoughts with feelings.

"Let go of these thoughts," the shaman said, "and listen to the inside, to your belly, which is the source of creativity, even before the mind."

Meanwhile, a male participant walked from the north to the center of the ring and danced like a clown, but his movements became extremely spastic, like an obsessive-compulsive neurosis, and it ended with him falling to the ground and having to calm down.

The woman standing in the southern part all the time—south stands for sensibility—was absent, even ignored, and when she, being irritated, tried to walk away out of the ring, the other women began to tell her, "You are wrong; you must participate. Your view on society is unrealistic."

Shortly thereafter, the male shaman got into a discussion with the female horse coach who accompanied the process "You do not consider the welfare of the horses—you do everything in your own way!" she told him. "You've got me out of my rhythm. I need my own way of working!"

But the shaman did not listen to her and kept telling people what they had to do in the field. The argument escalated so much that the shaman finally walked out of the field and did not want to participate anymore. Everyone looked confused; we could no longer see the meaning of this shamanic circle and decided that we just had to take a break to do it all over again.

It was only later that we realized that this was all part of the work in the big arena, and it symbolically showed the forces that are active in the present time, what tendencies there are and how to solve the disharmony in this field. The big field represents society, the world, or even the world of the living and the dead. On the whole, there are no boundaries, and everything is connected.

Intuitively, a group of men in the east—i.e., the direction of human action and energy—had formed in the end. They stood together in a row. The ladies talked to each other in a circle, and one said, "We have to go to the men to undo this division." But it was again discussed among the ladies. One said: "No, I'm not leaving," another woman: "Walking away does not make me feel understood." The more quiet one made a remark that she did not want to adapt to other people's expectations.

After a few minutes, the shaman came back and apologized. He had expected to just do the session the way he always worked; that was the rule, the protocol of his business practice. He was not used to working with horses and another coaching person at the same time.

"You always do everything your way," the coach said, more calmly this time, "but please do not interfere with my method! You are not considering the sensibility of the horses and these people!"

"I'm sorry," apologized the shaman. A long silence followed; even nature seemed not to make a sound for a moment. The shaman turned to the gentlemen, who stood beside him, without saying anything. The ladies, with the female coach in front, were a few steps away from the men's group.

There was a noticeable change when, suddenly, the shaman and then the rest of the men's group bowed before the ladies. It was an almost magical moment, and a wave of emotion went through the group. The ladies were moved to tears as the men bowed before them, as if all the misunderstandings were no longer important and the creative, sensible power of the feminine was honored and integrated in the existing field.

Thereafter, the ladies intuitively felt that they also had the space to bow, out of respect for the men's group. In this scene, the older mare suddenly stood next to us, and the other horses quietly distributed throughout the arena. Feeling a new harmony is something very invigorating. Words are then superfluous.

When the male, assertive, creative force in society is connected with the female, new possibilities emerge: management with empathy, protocols with communication, technology with creativity, digital systems with humanity, and no doubt a better, more joyful world, with more justice and sustainability.

Tranquility

THE OFFICE PARTY WAS in full swing; they made wishes for the upcoming holidays, and the whole team enjoyed a wonderful festive dinner. Even the somewhat introverted Walter had taken part in the dance that evening with his girlfriend.

The stressful atmosphere that had once existed in the company, with its individual teams, was gone. The conversation at the table had been lively, new contacts had formed, and absenteeism had declined generally in recent months.

Stephen stood on the terrace with his wife, and both looked at the park and the lights in the distance. The scent of autumn leaves and spruce was in the air.

Stephen felt much more relaxed than before; he had learned to delegate his tasks more and to have more confidence in the members of his team. He had learned to deal more with people than with the processes; sometimes he spontaneously had a friendly, easy conversation with the staff and showed personal interest in them. He discovered a totally new and interesting realm with it: there was one employee, who, just like him, loved the sea and was interested in boating technology, and another employee who had a special talent for designing new brochures.

And when there were problems with deliverables, the issues were discussed openly in the department, and they actively looked at how they could make it more optimal in the future.

They also had an exchange of ideas about initiatives that could be implemented, and they sat together in the relaxed atmosphere in front of the fireplace.

Dark and light

THE WORLD SUDDENLY SEEMED empty, like you could just turn back time and wipe out what happened, as if it had not happened at all! In March 2018, it did not stop raining in southern France. The paddocks of the horses flooded, because the water just would not drain off with that incredible amount of water. I tried to keep the horses, Quieto, Juan, and Olaf, regularly on a dry piece of land, but even the playground was a large swimming pool, with only a few dry spots.

Luckily the guys got some more grass during our ride and could at least dry their feet. Quieto, the oldest, seemed a bit tired from the weather and was just happy to get something out of our evening rides. I then had to leave for a few days. One day, they informed me that Quieto had broken out of his paddock. He would run with the other wild horses in the fields beyond the ranch and would nibble some grass with them.

The ranch owner had allowed him the "excursion" and wanted to wait to bring him back to his stable until the evening. Juan had stayed calm and apparently had no desire to go along.

I got a bit nervous in the evening. It was already getting dark, and I would feel better when I knew where the horses were. I called the ranch owner.

"Yes," his daughter said cheerfully. "I'll look for him."

For a long time, I heard nothing. After two hours, I received the terrible news that they had found him. He lay peacefully, sleeping like a fairy-tale horse in the grass, but life had vanished from him; he had apparently chosen a place to die in peace, between olive and birch trees, in the soft grass where there was no water. My friend … for twelve years … was not there anymore. It was a terrible and painful truth that I had to endure for a long time afterward.

Three months later, his fun-loving friend Juan followed him: during a thunderstorm, he was struck by a lightning bolt. It was in the shelter where Olaf was usually housed. Had he taken his place to protect him, to give him the opportunity to get my full attention and share more experiences with me? As I ran to Juan in panic and grief and saw him lying on the ground next to the tree, Olaf stood in front of me, trembling, and looked at me with questioning, sad eyes.

The world did not seem to be the same anymore. Whenever I see yellow forsythias, I think of the two happy white comrades from whom I learned so much and who had shown me the first amazing results of systemic coaching.

One evening I sat in the barn of the two in the grass. It was a sunny day, and everything was dry again; small birds and butterflies were everywhere now. The thought of these two was again very strong, and in the afternoon, quiet words suddenly came to me:

"Energy is never lost, and we are still there … we are so happy that we have been able to help with systemic coaching and your area of life. This is only the beginning! But there is so much more we can do for you humans; you have not discovered everything yet with which we horses can help you!

"If you pay more attention to your feelings and develop an eye for animals and nature, completely new possibilities will unfold! Focusing with mind and feeling; that's important. With trust and unconditional love, there will be room for something new to unfold."

"It is time ..., time for a new time!"

I felt warm and thanked my two friends and saw a majestic eagle high in the sky above me.

Bibliography

Areford, David. *The Art of Empathy: The Mother of Sorrows in Northern Renaissance Art and Devotion.* Lewes, UK: D Giles Ltd., 2013.

Bean-Raymond, Denise. *The Illustrated Guide to Holistic Care for Horses. An Owner's Manual.* Beverly, MA: Quarry Books, 2009.

Bloom, Paul: *Against Empathy: The Case for Rational Compassion.*, New York, NY: Ecco Press, 2016.

Botbol, Michel, and Nicole Garret-Gloanec. *L'empathie au carrefour des sciences et de la clinique—Colloque de Cerisy.* Montrouge : Doin, 2014.

Breadberry, Dr. Travis: Why You Need Emotional Intelligence Published on February 6, 2017 ????? page 11.

Brenninkmeijer, Alex, Dick Bonnkamp, Karen van Oven, and Hugo Prein. *Handboek Mediation.* The Hague, Netherlands: Sdu Uitgevers, 2016.

Brisch, Dr. Karl-Heinz (2014, June 21), personal interview with the Süddeutsche Zeitung. Munich, Germany. Retrieved from <https://www.khbrisch.de/media/brisch_sz_krippen_lawine_210614.pdf> October 2019.

Brisch: Empathie durch „Babywatching". Es muss nicht die eigene Mutter sein. (2015.05.20) Retrieved from <https://www.faz.net/ aktuell/feuilleton/familie/mehr-empathie-durch-babywatching-von-kindern-13603007.html>, January 2020.

Cassely, Jean-Laurent. *Le côté obscur de l'intelligence émotionnelle.* SLATE.fr (2014), Retrieved from https://www.slate.fr/life/81891/ cote-obscur-intelligence-emotionnelle, December 2019.

Chakrabarti, Shantanu. *Searching for Non-Western Roots of Conflict Resolution: Discourses, Norms and Case Studies.* New Delhi, India: K W Publishers Pvt. Ltd., 2013.

Christians, Clifford, and Michael Traber. *Communication Ethics and Universal Values.* Thousand Oaks, CA: SAGE Publications, 1997.

Eidelberg, Ludwig. *The Face behind the Mask.* Stuttgart, Germany: Hippokrates Verlag, 1948.

van Gestel-van der Schel, Nanda. *Het paard as spiegel van de ziel.* Heeten, Netherlands: Rozhanitsa, 2009.

Hallberg, Leif. *The Clinical Practice of Equine-Assisted Therapy: Including Horses in Human Healthcare.* New York, NY: Routledge, 2017.

Hoile, Penny. *Create a culture of working less hours and you'll boost productivity. Here's why.* SAGEpeople.com, 9 2020. <https:// www.sagepeople.com/about-us/news-hub/creating-culture-working-less-boost-productivity.>

Jandt, Fred E. *An Introduction to Intercultural Communication: Identities in a Global Community.* Thousand Oaks, CA: SAGE Publications, 2004.

Jones, Tiffany. *The Lack Of Emotional Intelligence In The Workplace Business Essay.* UKEssays.com. 11 2013. All Answers Ltd.

Bibliography

01 2020 <https://www.uniassignment.com/essay-samples/business/
the-lack-of-emotional-intelligence-in-the-workplace-business-essay.
php?vref=1>.

Juba, Brendan. *Universal Semantic Communication.* Berlin-Heidelberg,
Germany: Springer Verlag, 2011.

Kirby, Meg. *An Introduction to Equine-Assisted Psychotherapy: Principles, Theory, and Practice of the Equine Psychotherapy Institute
Model.* Bloomington, IN: Balboa Press, 2016.

Knaapen, Ruud. *Coachen met paarden.* The Hague, Netherlands:
Uitgeverij Boom en Nelissen, 2012.

Konir, Gerhard. *Horse-Based Coaching.* Norderstedt, Germany:
Books on Demand, 2012.

Lemstra, Boudewijn. *Eerste hulp bij organisatievraagstukken: de mogeli-
jkheden van systemisch werken in bedrijf en organisatie.* Austin, TX:
Brave New Books, 2016.

Lutz, Edith. *Grenzgänge im Januar: zwiaschen Iseal und Palästina.*
Berlin, Germany: AphorismA Verlag, 2008.

Nguyen-Phuong-Mai, Mai. *Intercultural Communication: An Inter-
disciplinary Approach: When Neurons, Genes, and Evolution Joined
the Discourse.* Amsterdam, Netherlands: Amsterdam University
Press, 2017.

Patterson-Kane, Emily Gay. *The Sensitivity of Animals and Applica-
tion of the Three Rs.* American Veterinary Medical Association,
Schaumburg, IL, altex.ch (2020). Retrieved from http://www.
altex.ch/resources/451454_Patterson21.pdf

Ramsbotham, Oliver, Tom Woodhouse, and Hugh Miall. *Contem-
porary Conflict Resolution.* Cambridge, UK: Polity Press, 2011.

Pletzer, Marc A. *Emotionale Intelligenz. Einführung und Trainings-
buch.* Freiburg, Germany: Haufe-Lexware Verlag, 2017.

Sachser, Norbert. *Der Mensch im Tier. Warum Tiere uns im Denken, Fühlen und Verhalten oft so ähnlich sind.* Hamburg, Germany: Rowohlt Verlag GmbH, 2018.

Sart, Gamze. *Emotional Intelligence in Peace and Conflict Resolution Education: Developing Peace Culture by Improving Emotional Intelligence.* Saarbrücken, Germany: LAP Lambert Academic Publishing, 2012.

Schafer, Svenja. *Educational Concepts on the Subject of Empathy Education Using the Film* David's Wondrous World. München, Germany: GRIN Verlag, 2016.

Schonewille, Manon A. *Toolkit Mediation.* The Hague, Netherlands: Boom Lemma Uitgevers, 2012.

Stange, Karlene. *The Spiritual Nature of Animals: A Country Vet Explores the Wisdom, Compassion, and Souls of Animals.* Novato, CA: New World Library.

Subramanian, Dilip, Bénédicte Zimmermann. *Voice in French corporate training: A critical issue in developing employee capability.* Journals. SAGEpub.com (2017), Retrieved from <https://journals.sagepub. com/doi/abs/10.1177/0143831X17704311>, February 2020.

Thomsen, Hans. *The Quantum World: Are animals observers in Quantum events?* Independently published, 2018.

Tolle, Eckhart. *The Power of Now: A Guide to Spiritual Enlightenment.* Novato, CA: New World Library, 1999.

Trujillo, Mary Adams. *Re-Centering Culture and Knowledge in Conflict Resolution Practice.* Syracuse, NY: Syracuse University Press, 2008.

Veenbaas, Wibe, Joke Goudswaard, and Henne Arnout Verschuren. *De maskermaker: systemisch werk en de karakter structuren.* Utrecht, Netherlands: Van Phoenix Opleidingen, 2015.

Volcic, Zala, Cindy Gallois, and Shuang Liu. *Introducing Intercultural Communication: Globe Cultures and Contexts.* Thousand Oaks, CA: SAGE Publications, 2010.

Why employee motivation is important and how to improve, measure and maintain it. Perkbox.com (2020) Retrieved from https://www.perkbox.com/uk/platform/insights/why-employee-motivation-is-important-and-how-to-improve-measure-and-maintain-it, January 2020.

www.ingramcontent.com/pod-product-compliance
Lightning Source LLC
Chambersburg PA
CBHW031154020426
42333CB00013B/658